THE FRIAR'S CURSE.

A LEGEND OF INISHOWEN,

OR,

DREAMS OF FANCY

When the Night was Dark.

BY

MICHAEL QUIGLEY.

MILWAUKEE:
Evening Wisconsin Printing House.
1870

INTRODUCTION.

In presenting this little volume to the patronage of my countrymen, I have only to state, that it was written after the exhaustive labors of the day, by the light of the lamp, as a means to divert the mind from the sterner trials of every-day life. Under more favorable circumstances it might have been less unworthy.

As it is, I am in hopes that many, who, like me, are debarred from visiting in person the far-off hills of holy Ireland, will accompany me, in imagination, to the rude but hospitable hearth of our native glens. To those familiar with the locality of the story, I hope they will deal gently with the inexperienced and untutored hand, that has thus attempted to portray from the tablets of memory—scenes worthy the pencil and genius of an artist, who could contemplate in person the grandeur of the landscape—

> "Till from the wondrous wild around,
> The soul her inspiration found."

The Friar's Curse.

CANTO FIRST.

The wintry day had closed in night,
Tho' not a star appeared in sight;
The rain fell cold, fierce blew the blast,
And gloom the face of heaven o'ercast,
When turning from the surging Foyle, [1]
His winter leggings splashed with soil,
And bending 'neath a cumbrous load,
A traveler takes the mountain road,
That clambering o'er the Cloghan lone,
Winds through the vales of Inishowen.
The gale that from the hill swept down,
At times the torrent's roar would drown;
Its pelting hail and blinding spray,
The trav'ler often held at bay;
But ever 'twixt each fitful surge,
His toilsome upward way would urge.
Now dipping in the deep ravine,
The tortuous path is scarcely seen;
Now o'er the treach'rous moor it bends,

Now cross the mountains breast ascends;
Now backward turns to shun some mass
Of rock that blocks the narrow pass;
Yet ev'ry step the traveler strode,
He seemed familiar with the road.
Soon darker shadows fall around,
The pathway climbs o'er icy ground,
As higher up the hill he wends,
He with more chilling gale contends;
The rain and hail he braved below,
Now fall around his track in snow,
Till weary, way-worn and oppressed,
He wanders on the mountain's breast;
His pathway lost, his vigor gone,
Benumb'd, confounded and alone.
May pitying heav'n in mercy bend,
And to his prayers an answer send.
We leave him lorn and in distress,
To view another's wretchedness,
Who at the closing of the day,
Traversed the self-same dreary way;
Contending with the mountain gale,
Ere yet our trav'ler left the vale;
Oft forced to turn, his breath to gain,
So fiercely swept the wintry rain;
And as he climb'd the mountain hold,
The shrieking wind grew fierce and cold;
The rain that drench'd him in the dale,
Now makes his cloak a coat of mail;
Adds to the burden of his woe,
Up in this land of ice and snow;

But his lithe limbs and youthful breast,
At last attain the mountain's crest;
Where on the Cloghan's summit high,
Seen dimly 'gainst the murky sky,
He seems the monarch of the waste,
On barren throne of ruin placed,
Stern guardsman o'er his rude domain,
Who knows no rival in his reign!
Now turning down a narrow dell,
Where soft as dew on holy well,
The snow among the heather fell,
Beneath a crag's projecting crown,
Awhile to rest he sits him down.
There came a lull amid the storm,
The crescent moon unveiled her form,
Threw on Glentogher's mountain stream,
A churlish, chilling, sickly beam,
But not enough of light to show,
Its wand'rings in the vale below;
Beneath the moon's dim light, display'd,
The scene the trav'ler now surveyed,
A scene so desolate and wild,
Had ne'er before his gaze beguil'd;
In heaven the tempest king unfurl'd
His stormy banner o'er the world,
And in his tyrant wrath and pride,
From earth the struggling beams would hide
His black battalions from afar,
Now mustering to renew the war;
Below Glentogher's giant base,
Lies dark as death—the eye may trace

Though vague and dim, his summit piled
Among the clouds, the torrent wild,
That erst in furious headlong pride,
Tore his rude breast and barren side,
Is borne upon the whirling blast,
From gale to gale in mockery passed,
'Til all congealed 'bove crag and dell,
Back on his naked head it fell.
Wreathing his frowning forehead now,
Like hoar-locks on a giant's brow,
Whilst 'mid this elemental strife;
No sound is heard of ought with life.
A rugged pathway's narrow span,
The only record left by man;
Short space the weary man delayed,
He rose, and from the friendly shade,
The dangerous track intently viewed;
And then its downward course pursued.
Whilst darkness closed around his way,
Fresh perils on his journey lay;
The arch of stone that spaned the gorge,
One half lies in the torrent's surge;
He climbs the ruin that remains,
The bank beyond in safety gains;
Again the snow-wreaths eddy round;
Again he hears the moaning sound,
The gathering tempest's pioneers
Heard, ere the conquering host appears:
More swift he hurries him along,
Awed by the thund'ring battle song.
'Mong wild Glentogher's barren hills,

The herald of a hundred ills,
The blinding snow his path blockades,
More fierce the ruthless gale invades,
When darkness, drift and freezing gale,
Amid these trackless wilds assail,
The mountain herd, his heart will quail.
The torrent that he crossed before,
He wanders to its brink once more ;
One tottering buttress stands alone,
The other, with the arch is gone.
Again the wanderer turns him back,
And steals along the torrents track,
Hoping to reach the narrow plain,
Along its banks, but all in vain.
A solid wall stands sentinel,
And bars his passage thro' the dell ;
The waters dash against the rock,
And turn aside so fierce the shock,
Fatigue his toiling limbs oppress ;
He sorrows o'er his ill success ;
And perils he can ill disguise,
Before his troubled soul arise ;
T'were well had I but turned aside,
Obedient to that older guide,
Nor rashly risked this mountain way,
When closed the threatening wintry day ;
He saw the tempest in the air,
And bade me of its wrath beware.
To tempt this angry stream were death,
To make my couch upon the heath,
With these fierce gales to freeze my blood,

Were fatal as the foaming flood;
I cannot climb this barricade,
My desperate peril who will aid?
He knelt him down, Oh! Heav'n, thy care,
My helpless wandering can repair;
Thy mercy and thy power alone,
Will shield me, else am I undone.
Fond Mother of the Son divine,
Thy pitying eyes on me incline,
If thou all spotless may abide,
A wandering child to sin allied.
Bright rose of bliss, fair lily flower,
Remember how in childhood's hour,
Ere pride or guilt had soiled the shrine,
Of my young heart, that heart was thine;
With sinless childhood's chaplet sweet,
I lay my sorrows at thy feet;
The garlands faded bloom restore,
And save thy wretched child once more;
And let his fainting soul find rest,
Again on thy maternal breast.
Whilst I—he raised his eyes above,
Renew to thee my early love.
Those tearful eyes at once behold,
A glory rare of burnished gold;
The driving clouds and angry rack,
That vail all heaven beside in black;
Touched by that fair aurora's ray,
Dissolve in light and die away.
Whilst yet he gazed the glory fled,
And blazed a beauteous star instead,

Beneath the star from sable shroud,
Of dark impenetrable cloud,
Up rose the fair young queen of night,
And poured on earth a flood of light;
Adorned in robes of virgin snow,
And smiling in the moonlit glow,
Far distant hills the scene expand,
A scene majestic, lovely, grand,
Whose chaste magnificence excels,
The naked grandeur of those dells.
But little marked our hero there,
That wintry scene surpassing fair;
The gale now leagued with fiercer cold,
Rang'd o'er the landscape uncontroll'd,
And scattered o'er the rude domain,
Like husbandman his garner'd grain;
The chilling snow thus broadcast spread,
Our trav'ler blinds at every tread;
Oft in some hidden gulch to sink;
Oft tottering o'er the torrent's brink,
As up the shelving rock he crawls,
Touched by his hand the boulder falls;
Descending now the icy glades,
The treacherous stay his foot evades;
Like angel from high heaven hurled,
He rushes to a nether world,
Half frozen, fainting and oppressed,
Hope flickers in his falt'ring breast;
Dread perils close on every side,
At last the frowing crags divide;
Rude record of some earthquake's birth,

When chaos rul'd primeval earth,
He struggled thro' the dark defile,
Hopes kindling rays his cares beguile,
Fresh vigor to his limbs restore,
The goal is won, his perils o'er!
Glentogher! all thy wilds are passed,
No more he feels thy chilling blast,
That wand'ring 'mong thy frozen dells,
Has chang'd his breath to icicles;
Above his head the beech trees high,
Nod in wild naked majesty;
Immortal ivy climbs the glades,
The mountain holly's leafy shades
On either hand in somber rows
Bestow the scene a soft repose;
A mellow radiance greets his gaze,
And 'mong the foliage sprinkles rays
Of amber light. Now pours a blaze
Of golden glory. Nestling near
Smiles cottage of some mountaineer,
Where vocal minstrelsy resounds,
And all his toilsome wand'rings crowns.
It was no frigid icicle,
That glowed and glistened as it fell;
The truant tear-drops stole away,
Warm tribute to the tender lay,
Whose potent charm his heart waylaid,
And at the porch his footsteps staid;
No wealthy mansion this, no hall
Of feudal lord whose warder's call,
Sends down the drawbridge o'er the moat,

For prince or pilgrim ; the thick coat
Of cozy thatch, and humble door,
Without a bar guard all more sure,
Than mote and bridge and embrazure,
Warder and watch-tower of the great,
Whose pomp of life and high estate,
Tho' bartered all can ne'er secure,
Such peace as oft surrounds the poor,
As dwelt within this cabin rude,
Far up the mountain's solitude ;
Within its cloister let us stray,
When closed that raw December day.
Ere yet our hero left the vale,
To struggle with the Cloghan's gale,
A matron reverend and serene,
And dignified as royal queen,
Whose clear blue eyes and modest grace,
Shine o'er a sweet benignant face,
Time's ruthless hand or early grief,
The flowers has crushed and sear'd the leaf,
And wintry ages gath'ring snows,
Among her once bright locks repose :
But yet through ev'ry charms decay,
Some radiance breaks of early day,
Like mountain fern whose bloom is gone,
The fragrance, with the stem, lives on ;
Her skillful hands the distaff dress,
With golden flax's silken tress,
A maiden lovely, past compare,
Like summer's rose as bright as rare,
Her dimpled cheeks and laughing eye,

O'erflow with dangerous witchery.
Her care the busy wheel supplies,
Now round her brow the fillet ties,
Her jetty ringlets crowd below,
In clusters round her breast of snow.
Bright Inishowen a form more fair,
Ne'er breathed thy healthy mountain air,
Nor lighter footsteps ever pressed,
Thy smiling valley's flowery breast,
Wo! worth the youth, who reckless strays.
Too near those charmed enchanting rays;
Alas, too late his heart may prove
Fair beauty's queen, the queen of love
Another youthful form we trace.
Tho' all concealed, the maiden's face,
A ponderous volume stained with age,
But rare illuminated page;
The cover clasped with golden bands,
The maiden holds in both her hands;
The modest 'kerchief cannot hide,
Her gentle bosom's swelling tide.
Within its sacred warm recess,
What treasure lie of tenderness,
Of feeling deep and pure, of truth
Ofall that bless or brighten youth;
In tones as sweet as silver bells,
Her tongue unfolds the chronicles,
Pours on each listener's raptured ear,
The glorious deeds recorded here;
Tales of renown and deeds sublime,
That royal bards in stately rhyme,

To Ulster's kings and nobles grand,
And chieftains of the northern land,
And courtly dames of beauty rare;
The high, the noble and the fair,
In princely halls on festal day,
Wed to the harps sweet minstrelsy;
Alas, that harp is now unstrung;
The heroes with the bards that sung,
Their triumphs, all have passed away;
The silent halls in cold decay,
In gloomy grandeur sad, sublime,
Great in their ruin war with time;
Tradition's dim recorded tale,
Or Keena of the funeral wail,
As clansmen to the house of clay,
Some sleeping chieftain bear away.
These failing witnesses alone,
Proclaim the glories of Tir own;
Her secptered kings of high renown,
And great Tirconell's deeds hand down,
The battles fought, the conquests won.
In vocal tales from sire to son;
In lay, in legend, prose and rhyme
All indistinct thro' mists of time,
Long did the maiden cheer that band,
With legends of the northern land,
Chief after chief in order fair,
Succeeds with deeds illustrious, rare.
Awhile she paused the page to scan,
And thus another tale began:
List gentles to a royal tale,

List to the legend of O'Neil,*
The pride of Erin's Kingly line,
The prop of every rightful throne,
Proud champion of her faith divine.
Attune your harps to cheer the song,
Fair ladies hearken to the tale;
Awake the glories that belong
To Ulsters pride, Owen Roe O'Neil.
She turned the leaf but silent gazed,
On page that much her soul amazed;
She pondered mute the mystic lore,
The more she read she wondered more,
Till from the book the scroll she drew,
And held it to the matron's view.
What are those words of mystery?
A riddle or a prophecy?
The matron answered yes my child,
They are a riddle dark and wild,
A prophecy of old—yea worse,
Called by the clans the Friar's Curse.
If for to-night thou wilt forgo,
The legend of the great Owen Roe,
I'll tell you of that mystic page,
Whose answers come from age to age,
And bid the clansmen still pursue,
The problems strange for answers true.
The maiden said 'twould please her well
Should she consent the tale to tell;
She closed at once the book of fame;
Read thou to me, replied the dame,

*Owen Roe O'Neal, king of Tiron.

The prophecy I'll fix once more,
My mem'ry on its mystic lore,
And to your wond'ring mind unroll,
Strange truths from that prophetic scroll.
The parchment page the maiden spread,
And these the wond'rous words she read:

THE FRIAR'S CURSE.

I.[2]

When from Strabreagy's briny wave,
The thirsty boatman stoops to lave
Sweet water from his barges side,
At anchor on the high spring-tide;
When ships shall in the clouds be seen,
And on the ocean forests green,
And men on wings of fire arise,
And fly triumphant thro' the skies;
These all shall be, not even then
Shall come a chief to rule the glen.

II.

When up huge cranny's dizzy side,
The huntsman on his steed will ride;
When Royal Oughie's reign is o'er,
And Faries flee from Goreymore,
When great Tirconnel's heirs will lie
In waning life's last agony,
And watchers o'er the chieftain fail,
To hear the faithful Banshee's wail;
All these shall be, not even then
Shall come the chief to rule the glen!

III.

When ocean from unfathom'd bed,
Restores to life the hidden dead,
That in its mighty depths profound,
Ten years and twice seven days lay bound;
When beauty, spotless as the dove,
And heaven shall bless, bestows true love
On man deformed, despoiled of grace,
And all unsought seeks his embrace;
When these appear to sons of men,
A chief will rise to rule the glen!
The curse of heaven, all others bans,
Who claim to rule the mountain clans,
Then shall the black wolf's cub explore,
The fairy dells of Goreymore
The lamb all innocent and mild,
That nestles in its native wild,
Shall with the wolf in sportive play,
Beguile the spring-time's bloom away;
And when the summer's fervent hour,
In blooming fragrance guilds the bower,
Seek covert in his ancient den,
The clans—O'Donnel of the glen
Shall rise to sway, but not till then!

Now childen, list! the matron said,
And of that scroll long held in dread
By all the clans, I'll trace the source,
And the occasion of the curse.

THE MATRON'S STORY.

I.

The summer sun in warm effulgent glow,
His early radiance shed o'er hill and plain;
Waking the dew-decked leaf and opening blow,
To fragrant life and beauty once again.
The lavrock in the heav'ns woke his retrain,
From the old hawthorn sung the mellow thrush;
And humbler songsters each in tuneful strain,
His matin lauds, poured forth from dell and bush,
And heaven's approving smile blest nature's virgin
flush

II

Beneath a spacious mansion by a hill,
That overlooked the broad Atlantic's shore,
Within its farthest chamber calm and still,
Stood a fair youth, an aged man before;
Unearthly fire burn'd in his eye, tho' hoar
His flowing beard and venerable hair,
I saw it then my child—its sick'ning gore [3]
My soul dismayed, and stain'd thy palm so fair;
Thus spoke the aged man, Oh! Cyher Roe, beware!

III.

Go kill a cock! [4] Last night at close of day
That deed I done. Choose from the snowy fold
A lamb of innocence, and ruthless slay
With anger fierce—with vengeance uncontroll'd—
The victim mute. When the bright sun uproll'd
His fiery chariot decked in robes of state,

At early prime with anger fierce and bold,
That innocent my hand did immolate;
Oh! Father look once more, what thou dos't see relate.

IV.

The aged man took hold the stripling's hand,
And to his reverend features it upraised;
Those secret signs no eye may understand,
With only mortal sight, on these he gazed;
His body trembled but his soul amazed,
The shadowy phantom silently pursued;
Alas, my son the angry fire that blazed,
At gloaming yesterday its crimson flood,
Illumes those deep canals where streams a kinsman's blood.

V.

Father, with faltering voice the youth began,
Is this dread deed my soul abhors—by fate,
Irrevocably sealed, I bear no man,
So heaven be witness, malice, grudge or hate;
If penances the guilt will expiate,
That to the unblest homicide belong,
And leave the deed undone, to me relate;
If prayer or fasts or unrelenting thong
Of self correcting discipline—or all—forbid the wrong.

VI.

To God's all-seeing eye the seer replied,
From all eternity—creations scroll—
The universe—the rebel Angels pride;
Those worlds unnumbered that thro' ether roll,

And worlds to come—man's being and his soul,
To his own image fashioned—man unborn;
What was, what is, what is to be, the whole
Is present! To man time's passing morn
Belongs. The time to come his vision laughs to scorn.

VII.

Save when the Almighty Being infinite,
In power and in perfection—prophecy,
On sons of men bestow. My second sight,
No inspiration knows no sanctity,
To-morrow's shadow cast upon the sky,
Of yesterday or to-day, an hour or more,
Ere time with his events come hurrying by,
A herald voice, a fugitive before
Proclaiming what time's torch to-morrow may explore.

VIII.

What I behold is not the dread event,
Or how or where, but lines that concentrate
Symbolic signs that dimly represent
As specters, men, the things that I translate,
Exists no seal unholy of fixed fate,
A deed to do --whether of good or ill;
Angels and man did God alike create,
To love him and adore—more wondrous still
Gave both alike dread power to work or thwart his will.

IX.

Our holy church with Matins, Mass and Lauds,
To-day Saint John's great festival doth bless;
Thou needest not disciplinary rods,

Nor hair cloth habit thou didst near transgress,
With thought impure: But go my son confess
To the physician of the soul thy care;
Lay open wide the heart's unseen recess;
Our deadly enemies oft ambush there,
To wound the unguarded soul in guise exceeding fair.

X.

[5]Pass thou this day at great Saint Columb's shrine,
And to calm contemplation yield thy soul;
Thy covenant to meet the clans resign,
Sad conflicts oft their gatherings control;
To Christ who thee redeemed—increase thy toll;
The son of God who died upon the tree,
This promise made, who alms bestows or dole,
Upon the poor on earth but gives to me,
Him heaven will all repay with triple usury.

XI

Young Cyher did his reverend sire obey,
Made his souls shrift as often he had done;
And 'mong the poor and lowly knelt to pray,
Till past meredian was the summer sun;
And many a needy pilgrim's blessing won,
For generous largess to relieve their need;
Oh! had he finished all so well begun,
Heaven had not witnessed the appalling deed;
Nor heard the affrighted soul its gory issue plead.

XII.

[6]Where Donagh's granite crosses gray with age,
Stand witnesses of Erin's faith divine;

Mocking the fierce despoiler's vandal rage,
Whose wanton fury overturned the shrine,
And broke the stone and blurr'd the sacred line,
The holy legend of the honored dead,
High on the hill above of rude design,
A lofty cairn of stone uprear'd its head,
But for what purpose rais'd, tradition no t hing said.

XIII.

As is the usage still, so was it then ;
Four times within the circle of the year
A Fair to hold. From village, dale and glen,
The mountain clans were wont to muster here ;
The maiden fair, the youthful mountaineer,
Here made their trysting place by tender plight ;
The women all in scarlet cloaks appear,
The men in gay attire, a morn more bright,
The sun of June ne'er warm'd. Alas ! how dark the night.

XIV.

The clans of Malin, from its farthest shore,
By Phelim Dhu O'Doherty were led ;
Where wild Glen Tuscar, barren, bleak and hoar,
Repels the wave and rears his frowning head ;
A stalwart race upon the ocean bred,
Fierce as its wave McLaughlin More obeyed,
Young Cyher Roe his aged sire instead,
From Carramore to Knockamanny swayed,
These to the cairn that day, without a leader stray'd.

XV.

Altho' it was their very souls desire,

And dearest wish there boy-chief there to view;
Proud of his comely grace and manly fire,
That sparkled in his thoughtful eye of blue;
Tho' he his former plight did late renew,
On yes'ter eve beside the Baelfire's glow;
His absence every clansman urged, was due
To filial love, like current choked with snow,
So in his reverend sire life's stream flowed cold and low.

XVI.

Loud merriment around the cairn that day,
Assumed her gayest robes and richest cheer;
Beneath the tents the pipes loud minstrelsy,
Inspired the joyous dance or pleased the ear,
High on a wooden stage with sword and spear,
And decked in motley guise, a strolling band
Of swarthy gypsies filled the young with fear;
Now poised an anvil on a hazel wand,
And words of magic spoke that unseen powers command.

XVII.

There too assembled 'mong that happy throng,
A band detested, to no clan allied,
Who lawless, reckless, turbulent and strong,
Obeyed a captain fierce, a man of pride;
Feardarrig named, of giant strength and stride,
His house upon the summit of Ardmore,
It windows opened to the Atlantic wide,
The weary beggar shunned its cheerless door,
Nor dared his nearest kin the dark abode explore.

XVIII.

For thro' the country round spread horrid tales,
Of this dread captain and his secret land;
How, when the vessel tossed, mid tempest gales,
With signal guns, alarmed the sleeping land;
False beacons blazed on Polon's beach of sand,
And torches waved from Carrick's castles old;
Inhuman hearts, foul midnight murder plan'd,
The stranded ship, the corpses grim and cold,
And the fierce wreckers near, the damning tale unfold

XIX.

The bright midsummer sun tho' coursing down,
Ruled like a monarch proud, his realm on high;
When rose a gallant cheer, whose echoes drown
The boisterous mirth and pipes loud minstrelsy;
The distant loiterers hear the exultant cry,
And swell the crowd that sways from side to side;
Hats wave in air, and scarfs and 'kerchiefs fly,
Welcome fair Cyher Roe, each clansman cried;
Long live the son of Con—prop of his house and pride!

XX.

Who cares for Con? or for his house's hope?
Or them who swell their lungs with silly praise?
From all his mountain clans find one to cope
With bold Feardarrig, who no chieftain sways;
Free as the wind wher'er he lists he strays,
Alike untrammel'd on the sea and land;
He pays no chiefry, works no duty days,

But guards his own with strong and steadfast hand,
And Cyher Roe defies, and all his boasting band.

XXI.

Bold man, forbear! the youthful chief replied;
Clans of the mountain glens list what I say;
Heed not these mutterings of this son of pride,
Nor desecrate this hallowed festal day;
Nor mar its mirth and blithsome revelry,
With hostile speech and unbecoming strife.
O'Donnell of the glen thy wrath allay,
This desperate man but thirsts for human life,
Else why on day like this come armed with deadly knife.

XXII.

False, cried Feardarrig, this I always wear,
On every day and whereso'er I go;
'Tis my companion in my midnight prayer,
'Twill help a friend as well as harm a foe
With this I had not thought to strike a blow,
Unless by steel opposed, I did intend,
With this my trusty staff to overthrow,
Your bravest man. His knife he gave a friend,
And swung his staff around, his challange to commend.

XXIII.

Then Hugh O'Donnel known, as Hugh the strong,
Broke thro' the crowd. Let all a circle clear,
As first of kin. he cried, be mine the wrong,
To right at once, let no one else come near;
I claim no vantage by my clansmen here,

Save what the laws of honor may proclaim;
These to the mountain clans are ever dear;
[7]Strike son of Denmark for thy father's fame,
I for my chief and clans; who fails his be the shame.

XXIV.

Then both in angry conflict crossed their staves,
Their bosoms filled with wrath, their looks with fire;
And long each furious adversary braves,
The blows impelled by rage and fierce desire,
From every pore the combatants perspire,
The sweat of toil, and oft the blinding spray,
Whilst with the sudden shock they back retire,
With hasty hand are fain to brush away;
Long did the struggle last and doubtful seemed the fray.

XXV.

Now stream their faces with a sea of gore;
Now falls Feardarrig on the flinty rock,
Now gains his feet, fierce as his race of yore,
And hurls his foeman back with mighty shock;
Young Cyher Roe the shepherd of his flock,
Fear'd not the issue of the desperate fight;
But fear'd Feardarrig's friend whose grinnings mock
O'Donnel's vantage. Him he kept in sight;
The knife in his clenched hand, his brow as black as night.

XXVI.

Feardarrig once again reels to the ground,
His staff high hurled from out his faithless hand;
Then leaped his comrade with an instant bound,
And gave his captain back the naked brand,

To foil the treacherous deed—the murder plann'd,
  The watchful chieftain like a greyhound sprung,
And ere the ruffian could his own command,
  He snatched it from his girdle where it hung,
  And back against the crowd the treacherous villian
    flung.

XXVII.

A whistle shrieked—the wrecker's signal blast,
  Their captain's peril to his band conveyed,
Borne on the tempest's wings less fierce, less fast
  The snow wreath flies—than they his need to aid,
Like mountain wolf, whose covert dogs invade,
  Feardarrig scan'd the circle from his lair,
His growl of rage and instant bound betrayed,
  His purpose dread, he raised his knife in air
  And sprang at Cyher Roe with vengence of despair.

XXVIII.

As speeds the arrow from the springing bow,
  As from the frowning cloud, the lightnings dart,
The supple stripling sprung upon the foe,
  His deadly weapon level'd at the heart;
The giant gave a quick spasmodic start,
  His mighty bosom's unabated force
Did to the youth such sudden shock impart,
  He fell beneath the grim and ghastly corpse,
  His garments drenched with blood, his bosom with
    remorse.

XXIX.

'Twere long to tell the struggle that ensued,
  Around the wrecker's carcass where it lay,
The rock was slippery with a mingled flood,

From friend and foe who shared the dread affray;
The clansman faint and mained was borne away,
Where wife or sister might his needs attend,
But where the wrecker fell he sank a prey
To unrelenting vengence, with no friend
To bind his grievous wounds, or mercy to commend.

XXX.

Their captain dead, surrounded by a race,
When roused to vengence, or impelled by rage,
Unpitying, cruel, drove from place to place.
Yet long that band did bloody warfare wage,
Tho' unavailing one would ten engage,
No hope of succor and no way to flee,
Nor pitying heart their sufferings to assuage;
One after one in dread extremity,
Lay round the cairn that day, a woeful sight to see!

* * * * * * *

XXXI.

Above the broad Atlantic's western wave,
The sun in softened splendor holds his way;
No sounds of strife, no cruel knife and stave,
The echoes startle or defile the ray;
The tuneful thrush awakes his vesper lay,
The black-bird answers with his whistle shrill,
And charming songsters make sweet minstrelsy;
On leaf and flower heaven's evening dews distil;
All nature smiles around that mansion by the hill.

XXXII.

Within the self-same chamber sits the seer,
A man is kneeling by the sage's knee;

His hands are clasped in agony or fear,
  His soul immersed in grief's extremity;
Attired in gown and hood, he seems to be
  A palmer, young, prepared for pilgrimage;
A girdle round his waist. A rosary
  And silver crucifix his gaze engage,
  But his o'erwhelming woe, appear not to assuage.

XXXIII.

The boat lies ready on the beach of sand,
  Soon will the rising tide her timbers buoy;
Her helm has oft obeyed thy skillful hand,
  Then haste away, my child, my age's joy,
Law's stern decretals may thy life destroy;
  In Innis Tory thou canst safely dwell,
Secure from penal rod—or worse annoy
  Of ruffian bandit's rage—heaven will dispel
  *The guilt thy soul affright's in Columb Kill's rude cell.

XXXIV.

Father! I beg thy benison. His hands
  Upon the anguished brow the old man laid;
May he whose just decree foul murder bans,
  Restore thy guiltless soul its peace betrayed;
And she, the sinner's refuge, sweetly aid
  Thy path of peril, and illume thy way;
Heaven sanctify the sorrows that invade
  A father's breast, to bless thee night and day;
  Go! but return to close my life's last flick'ring ray.

* * * * * * *

XXXV.

Ten weary years on time's revolving wheel,
  Have writ their chronicles of joy and pain ;
When to the aged chief the clans appeal,
  As oft they had before, and all in vain ;
Lest tyrant death life's title might arraign,
  But feebly held within his bosom old;
Since of his son no tidings he can gain,
  His house, his clans, his honor to uphold,
  That he appoint his heir, his name and rights unfold.

XXXVI.

Go! cried the aged chieftain, bring to me
  The holy friar, who by Strabreagy's shore,
[9]Within his cell of stone, in sanctity
  And solitude has passed seven years and more.
To him alone. No witnesses before,
  Shall I impart the secret you demand ;
When to my father's house you me restore,
  And lay me in my narrow cell of sand,
  That friar, your chief will show, all others shall be banned.

XXXVII.

They brought the holy friar that very night,
  And showed the chamber where the chieftain lay ;
But ere he entered he did all invite
  To bid their chief farewell and haste away,
That he beside his bed might watch and pray,
  And minister medicaments he knew
Would cheer the soul. None dared to disobey ;
  Each faithful clansman bade a sad adieu,
  And to his own abode, oppressed with grief, withdrew.

XXXVIII.

He bade the household servers all retire,
  Forbidding them his vigils to invade;
Himself would trim the lights and tend the fire,
  And if in need of help, would seek their aid.
In his coarse gown of sable serge arrayed,
  The hood so close that none his face might see,
The barefoot friar his noiseless steps essayed,
  Beside the chieftain's couch he bent the knee,
  And from his hallowed lips broke Benedicite.

XXXIX.

What makes the seeming sleeper sudden start?
  Why mutely gaze upon the palmer there?
Why flows life's current quicker thro' his heart?
  Ask you a father's love, it may declare,
His soul is busy with a silent prayer;
  The tears are coursing down his reverend face,
My guileless child, my Cyher Roe, the fair;
  It is his voice I hear, his form I trace.
  Father! the pilgrim spoke, and sought his Sire's embrace.

* * * * * * *

XL.

There is no breeze disturbs the ocean's rest,
  No angry waves the wintry shore assail;
No torrent rushes down old cranny's breast;
  Whence comes that murmur, like a moaning gale?
It is the song of woe, the funeral wail,
  That wakes the echoes of the lonely hill;
For Con, the mild, is borne along the vale,

The hand is cold, the generous heart is still,
And all the mountain clans are grieving o'er the ill.

XLI.

The coffin draped, as well becomes a chief,
Is on the shoulders of his kinsmen borne;
The reverend priest, his bosom dark with grief,
In stole and surplice leads the sage's urn;
An chants a sacred psalmody. In turn
The choristers awake the solemn song;
Behind the bier, a Monk, alone, forlorn,
Masked in his cowl, and barefoot steals along,
Then all the mountain clans, great unnumbered throng.

XLII.

In consecrated ground his bed they made,
Where from long ages past his fathers' rest;
Then, in the lonely house the coffin laid,
But ere they dropped the mold upon his breast,
The priest of God, the holy monk addressed,
And to the assembled clans, bade him unroll
Their honored chieftain's will and last bequest;
Each jot and tittle, largess gift and dole,
The truth, and all the truth, as God would search his soul.

XLIII.

Then spoke the holy Friar. Ere I declare
Your dying chieftain's sacred true decree;
Pledge me above his body lying there,
That from the judgment none shall disagree;
Men of the mountain clans swear this to me,
Before your living priest and leader dead;

And unclosed sepulchre—so shall it be,
  We swear it all—each clansman bared his head,
  And knelt—whilst to the throng the friar this judgment read.

XLIV.

I, Con O'Dougherty, sometimes called the mild,
  Chief of the mountain clans, by usage old;
By the full circle of my days beguiled,
  In peace with God, by holy church control'd;
Of all my faculties possessed: Unfold
  What here is writ upon this parchment scroll;
And seal it with our ancient seal of gold,
  To God's eternal love bequeath my soul,
  To dust my body give—my worldly goods thus dole.

XLV.

As next of kin, to Hugh O'Donnel Strong,
  Since I have lost my only son and heir,
My house and herds and holdings all belong,
  So he keep church and grave-yard in repair;
And of his fulness give the needy share,
  Who ask a shelter, or a help require;
All duty days,[10] all chiefry hence forbear,
  Such as were paid to me and to my sire,
  With me, and for all time these usages expire.

XLVI.

The priest, whoe'er he be, shall have a home
  Within the household, be it high or low;
By day and night, he will be free to come,
  By night, or day, unquestioned he shall go;
But when my body in the grave lies low,

And my poor soul has left its house of clay
Lest it too long in purgatorial woe,
By stains of earthly grossness make delay,
That priest for me one year a monthly mass shall say.

XLVII.

To Hugh and to his heirs for ever more,
Those rights and obligations I entail;
As from long years our fathers have before,
From sire to son. Nor shall possession fail
Our ancient stock—'til evil days prevail,
And heirs unjust our pandects violate;
God, this forbid, Amen! Alas the tale,
No smiles of welcome—Priest or poor await,
For strangers hands no close the once hospitable gate.

XLVIII.

When ceased the Friar, an angry murmur rose,
And all who knelt, their feet at once regain;
Tell us our future chief, his name disclose,
They cry aloud. The friar replied, arraign
The faulty record, nor of me complain,
All that is writ I read—we all agree;
Once more they cry, thy judgment to maintain,
Behold! we swear it each on bended knee!
Name thou our future chief, and when his rule shall be.

XLIX.

Pay the last tribute to your chieftain cold,
Fill up his grave, I will a while retire
Within the hallowed temple, and unfold
Before the God of wisdom your desire;

And beg his high omnipotence inspire,
My faultering tongue to glorify his name.
When he again came forth, celestial fire
Flamed in his eyes, awe stricken with the beam,
All knelt, and heard the friar that prophecy proclaim.

The mountain clans at once disperse,
In sorrow at the Friar's Curse;
All plighted to the dread decree,
This tale my mother told to me:
She from her sire the legend won,
And he from his, so did it run
Thro' old traditions, to the source
That gave the clans the Friar's Curse.
As years, their mysteries unroll,
Light beams around the mystic scroll;
Where shines the hill of Doon so fair,
[11]Three holy wells are flowing there;
Up from the sea beach bubbling still,
Their waters healing balm distill;
And like Bethsaidas blessed spray,
The pious pilgrim's ills allay.
When flows the ocean's briny tide,
Resistless in its power and pride;
Like Erin's faith, these wells endure,
Their waters rise o'er wave impure;
There boat-men drink—this wond'rous boon,
Still sanctifies the wells of Doon.
[12]Brazil's from Ballyhillion's ben,
Oft filled with awe sea-faring men;
Forest and glade, a landscape wide,
Where flowed below—the Atlantic tide.

[13]And Donnah Dearrig learn'd and wise,
Says those fierce meoters of the skies
Are firey chariots, madly driven
By magic art, in spite of heaven.
[14]Last Hallow Mass, a huntsman bold,
His steed o'er Cranny's breast controlled.
[15]Benevnue's, Fairy King, they say
Slew Oughie on that awful day,
When from the hills the herds were driven;
And clashing swords were heard in heaven,
And blood, fell from the clouds like rain,
And drenched and dyed the ripen'd grain;
Our guardian Fairies gained the day,
And drove Benevnue's hosts away;
But with such grief their Monarch mourned,
To Goreymore they ne'er returned.
That year my mother's brother died,
My uncle saw be-deck'd in pride,
[16]A specter ship, her sails unfurled,
On voyage to the spirit world,
And tho' a true born, proud O'Neill,
[17]No Banshe gave her warning wail,
And not a sound disturbed the dell,
The night his spirit bade farewell.
No Kena rose on Gorey's side,
When he, my only brother died;
Drumcroy's echoes silent lay,
When Shane, the gentle passed away;
[8]Tho' Kelly's wraith was seen in Drung,
And loud the warning hammers rung;
And thrice a bell was heard to toll

At midnight for McLaughlin's soul;
And all that week on Killian Brae,
The Banshe wailed the brave McRae.
Mother, fair Ellen cries, forbear!
The wind sighs wild, the night is drear;
Thy cheerless tale of death and doom,
My heart affrights and fills with gloom;
Till morning shines, the rest withhold,
Such tales in day-light should be told;
Let's wile the lonely night away,
With song of love. Now list my lay:

SONG.

I.

With the fragrance of summer the mild breeze is laden,
The thrush and the linnet in melody vie;
Yet richer the breath of my own lovely maiden,
No music so sweet as her soft-swelling sigh;
Oh! where dost thou tarry so long from thy lover,
Fond hope of my longing, my darling, my dear;
The turtles are cooing in yonder green cover;
Ah! why my own loved one, why art thou not here.

II.

The bright beaming sun o'er the landscape is smiling,
The lily is drooping in sweetness below;
In the lake's crystal mirror its beauty beguiling,
In vain to compare with thy bosom of snow;
The rose is unfolding its splendor and power,
As queen of the valley thy rights to invade;
Then hasten my lily, my own matchless flower,
And sham'd by thy brightness, thy rivals will fade.

III.

The sun cannot banish the clouds that hang o'er me,
  Despoiled of thy smile, all is sadness and gloom,
My heart will not own the gay prospect before me,
  If thou be not near me, my heart to illume;
Then come to me, dearest, the woodbine is weaving
  Its emerald canopy spangled with gold;
The bower is all fragrance, where lonely and grieving,
  I make my sad plaint, and my sorrows unfold.

IV.

Oh! come, and the beam of thy love-light will guide me,
  Where murmurs the brook in the mountain ravine;
Where primroses grow, with my charmer beside me,
  I'll pledge my allegiance and own her my queen:
The shadows of sadness will chill me no longer,
  If thou wilt attend to a true lover's tale,
And bless the fond heart whose pulsations grow stronger,
  As blooms in perfection the pride of the vale.

The maiden ceas'd—as with a moan,
The tempest struck the walls of stone;
The roof-tree creak'd beneath the press,
And all within their fears confess;
Low down upon the cabin floor
They kneel, and heavenly aid implore;
And to the Virgin still prolong,
Their fond appeal in tender song.

HYMN TO THE VIRGIN.

I.

Virgin Mother! maiden holy,
 Pure, immaculate and bright,
Hearken to us sinners lowly,
 Be our guardian fair this night;
Wicked still, and still transgressing,
 Mother! we appeal to thee;
Thou all sanctity possessing,
 Maiden, spotless! pray for me.

II.

Holy Mother! when before us,
 Pleasure's path is shining bright,
Be thou watching sweetly o'er us,
 Lest we're dazzled by its light;
When our bosom's faint or languish,
 Helpless all, to fight or see,
Aid our weakness, cheer our anguish,
 Maiden, spotless! pray for me.

III.

Aid us sinners, holy Mother!
 To repentance, when we fall;
Teach us wild desire to smother,
 God, our love, should be our all.
Queen of angels, queen of Heaven!
 Mournest thou our faults to see?
Sue that we may be forgiven,
 Maiden, spotless! pray for me.

The gale its frightful rage withdrew,
Though sad it moan'd and wildly blew ;
The gentle maids, their peril o'er,
Resumed each place they graced before;
The matron kneeling still delayed,
Whilst fancy early scenes portrayed;
There is a sweet, yet mournful joy,
Time softens, but can ne'er destroy,
To those whose heart's chords have been torn,
By death's rude grasp, in life's fair morn;
In wandering o'er, tho' all alone,
The scenes that both have gazed upon.
When home with early love is lost,
And the lone heart 'mong strangers tossed
In distant land, no more may view
Its native mountains mellow blue;
There is a bliss in wandering back,
In fancy, o'er life's flowery track,
In some fair glen or primrose dell,
Love's tale again we list or tell;
Along some streamlet's flow'ry maze,
The lover with the loved one strays ;
Or blest o'er all the world beside,
He greets in joy his blushing bride.
Thus, thus thro' life the heart will cling,
To its lost treasure: Wandering
O'er scenes long past and gleaning bliss,
Yea, all but love its self from this;
Young hearts no backward track explore,
Their wistful longings run before,
And bid the mind, in fair disguise,

Behold its future prospect rise.
The path of love fair flowers adorn,
Unfeared the chasm, unseen the thorn ;
And as it climbs life's upward slope,
At ev'ry turn fresh vistas ope,
And charming scenes the view expand,
Around the dreamer's fairy land.
Dream on, fair girl, thy dream of joy,
In fancy paint thy absent boy,
Contending with the mountain gale,
To reach his treasure in the vale.
Such thoughts in Ellen's breast arise,
And move the fount that moists her eyes ;
Still darker shades are gathering now,
And flit like clouds across her brow,
And fill her soul with gloom and fear,
" Hope of my heart, would he were here !"
Ah ! faithless lips, that thus confessed
The secret treasured in the breast ;
Ah ! tell-tale blushes, why proclaim
The guilty truth, with crimson flame ;
Tho' Cahir was Glentogher's pride,
And tarried oft by Ellen's side ;
Yet Ellen deemed to them alone,
The tender plant they nursed was known ;
The plant of love, whose bloom controls,
Whose fragrant tendrils bind their souls ;
That modest blush sheds o'er her face,
A beam of such bewitching grace,
As lends her charms far more of power,
Than owned they in their brightest hour.

Thus Sol in the meridian sky,
Blinds with his brightness every eye,
And scorches with his dazzling flame,
Like passion, all who dare the beam ;
But let the evening's crimson veil,
His blinding glory part conceal ;
The eye and heart alike repay,
The meed withheld, the prouder ray ;
Ellen, her former peace to win,
Bends o'er her wheel and tries to spin ;
With sweetest song the cabin rings,
But 'tis not blushing Ellen sings.

SONG.

I.

When tempests roam among the hills,
  And thro' the glens the gales career ;
When treach'rous snow the valley fills,
  And guiding stars all disappear ;
When o'er the Cloghan's mountain height,
  The wanderer dares the trackless dell,
What magic ray defies the night ?
  What beacon guides, can any tell ?

II.

When youthful maidens sing and sigh,
  And gloom usurps the throne of bliss,
And tears suffuse the radiant eye,
  Methinks there's something sure amiss ;
How can the lips the heart unlock ?
  The key lies hidden in the well ;

What magic powers our secrets mock?
  Say, blushing maids, can any tell?

III.

Oh! there's a little roguish child,
  With just enough of speech to lisp,
Who guides the wanderer o'er the wild
  In safety, with his will o' wisp;
The dew shook from his amber wings,
  Will moist the eye; and his the spell
Unlocks the bosom's secret springs;
  What is his name, can any tell?

When first the song met Ellen's ear,
She stopped her wheel, and paused to hear;
Her head against the distaff pressed,
And soft emotions swayed her breast;
The voice was sweet, and sweet the air,
The lay was light, the maid was fair;
But whilst the minstrel's queries rise,
A mirror dazzles Ellen's eyes,
And images unfold to view,
Within her breast the answers true;
Then coming footsteps softly fell,
And broke the singer's charming spell,
And foremost to love's watchful ear,
Proclaim the welcome wanderer here;
Light as a fawn's in forest glade,
Were the free foosteps of the maid,
Nor oped the charmed cave more free,
To robber's magic sesame,
Than oped the door to Ellen's art,

With welcome sent from lips and heart;
Nor quicker o'er the dewy lawn,
At sound of danger flees the fawn,
Than Ellen, when the stranger true,
To welcome spoke, appeared in view;
In sooth, it was a sight to make
Unwarned the stoutest bosom quake;
A saint in such fantastic guise,
Might counterfeit the king of lies;
His cloak once clothed the shaggy bear,
Now icicles adorned each hair,
And dangling lightly to and fro,
Like spangles caught the ingles glow:
A cap of fur, of darksome hue,
Like mask, his features hid from view;
Whilst leggings of the dundeer's hide,
A housing for his limbs supplied;
And gauntlets on his hands displayed,
Of saffron dye—such contrast made
As gave his form a savage mien,
Whilst silent he surveyed the scene;
He marked each denizen's alarm,
And fain their idle fear to charm,
In tones that soothed each troubled breast,
To Ellen first, his speech addressed.
Fair girl, I mourn my presence here,
Inspires thy gentle breast with fear;
A stranger, I, from foreign strand,
Bewildered in this mountain land;
With toil oppressed, benum'd with cold,
A helpless wight in me behold;

Whilst faltering in the dell below,
I gained this cabin's cheerfull glow,
And found in thee, an angel bright,
To welcome me to life and light;
Tho' for another dearer friend,
Was meant the welcome thou dids't send;
Yet, not more real the blessings shed,
By Israel old on Jacob's head,
Deeming his favorite Esau there;
Than thine to me, my lovely fair;
The maiden's cheeks with blushes burned,
When he to greet the matron turned,
Mother, an uninvited guest,
Weary and faint I plead for rest,
And heaven that sees my urgent need,
Forbids that I should idly plead.
The matron gave her kindly hand
And made him welcome to her band;
Tho' unexpected, thus you come,
Thou'rt welcome to our humble home;
Children! she said, be thine the care,
In haste the evening meal prepare;
The stranger's need my aid demands,
She plucked the gaunlets from his hands,
And chafed the palsied palms with snow
Till with reviving life they glow;
His cloak upon a beam she spread,
Undid the covering off his head,
And gathering in his wandering hair,
Left his bright cheek and forhead bare.
A cheek that hardly own'd the down

Of manhood—burnished well nigh brown,
With ray more fierce than ever fell
On Erin's mountain lake or dell.
And brow as open and serene,
As any in her island green.
And form whose perfect symmetry,
The sculptor's model well might be,
Such form, young maidens seldom flee,
Then in a chair by artist rude,
Hewn from the fir tree underwood,
With comfort fraught, but wanting grace
She bade the stranger take his place;
Forget my child, thy perils passed,
The mountain path and ruthless blast,
Let care thy youthful bosom flee,
And deem a mother smiles in me.
A tear stood in the stranger's eye,
His bosom swelled with grateful sigh,
And words of thanks all faltering came
To recompense the kindly dame.
Now, round the smiling board are pressed,
The matron, maiden's and their guest;
The matron with a housewife's care
Excuses oft their homely fare;
And maids abashed to eat before,
The stranger, wish the supper o'er;
Whilst he keen hunger's fierce desires
Fulfils; then from the board retires!
The supper past in quiet mirth,
They circle all around the hearth,
Willing to cheer the stranger's care,

Ellen awakes a lively air;
The stranger owns some secret spell,
As Mary joins the chorus swell.

SONG.

Grieve not stranger youth, to roam
  From thy scenes of childhood;
Thou shalt soon behold thy home,
  Cottage, brook and wild wood;
When returning from afar,
  Native mountain's greet thee,
Mellowed by the evening star,
  Think what joys will meet the.

CHORUS.

Churlish hearts may yield to sorrow,
  Ours, no cankering care shall borrow;
Smiles to-day, and sighs to-morrow,
    This our motto be

II.

Dost thou miss a father's aid
  In thine hour of danger;
Friends will rise if foes invade,
  Doubt not gentle stranger.
Kindly dames shall come to cheer,
  Tender hands sustain thee,
Lest thy bosom yield to fear,
  Or care or sorrow pain thee.

CHORUS.

III.

Mournest thou for eyes that shone,
  'Neath the shady cover,

Voice that charmed with tender tone,
  Lips that blessed her lover ;
Ever, Ever faithful prove,
  Ever, Ever, Ever.
Doubt thee not thy absent love ;
  Never, never, never.
Chorus.

IV.

Him, she chose in youths fond hour,
  Absence still makes dearer;
Painting with its magic power,
  Charms unseen when nearer ;
Joys untold her swain will bless,
  When her eyes behold him,
To her heart with fonder press,
  Will her arms enfold him.
Churlish hearts may yield to sorrow,
Ours, no cankering care shall borrow;
Smiles to-day, and sighs to-morrow,
    This our motto be.

The cheerful song was sung in vain,
Perhaps it woke with keener pain,
Feelings that might have dormant lain;
Memories of a tond one dear,
With face as fair, and voice as clear,
Whose past endearments wake again,
In tribute to the sweet refrain ;
At times a hidden glance he stole,
And in the look bestowed his soul

On her whose eyes delicious blue,
Whose riper charms attract his view;
As often sought the troubled swain,
Communion with himself again,
Till his young brow is clouded o'er
With darkling shades, unseen before!
The Matron marked his rising care,
And bade her guest for sleep prepare;
Then following where her footsteps led,
The wanderer finds a welcome bed;
Soon home's sweet blessings bright and warm,
The dreamer's midnight visions charm;
He hears the voice of neighbors old,
He grasps the hands of comrades bold,
With modest blush, the maidens coy,
Breathe welcome to the wandering boy!
But dearer still the fond caress,
Of one, whose smile alone can bless;
Oh! be thou soon restored fond swain,
To home, and friends, and love again;
And be thy waking bliss as bright,
As those fair visions of the night.

Now silence reigns, and spreads her pall,
O'er cottage, matron, maids and all;
The winds retire, the tempest sleeps,
The muse her lonely vigils keeps;
Poor muse! unknown to wealth or fame,
Without a patron, friend or name;
Sad muse! who by the embers glare,
Sees phantoms in the murky air,

With talons fierce and scorpion sting,
To wound the tongue that dared to sing;
Adieu, fond muse! may morn proclaim
Thy midnight spectres all a dream.

END OF FIRST CANTO.

THE FRIAR'S CURSE—CANTO SECOND.

[1]Slieve Snaght, 'tis thine by lofty claim,
To herald days returning beam,
As 'tis his last farewell to own,
Queen mountain fair of Inishowen.
And now in heavenly radiance bright,
We see you greet the wooing light ;
Whilst humbler hills and vales below,
Sleep 'neath their robes of virgin snow.
But Empress proud, deem not for thee,
Alone he comes ; as fair as free,
His smile will soon awake the plain,
To labor, life and light again.
Hark ! 'tis the huntsman's mellow horn,
Awakes the echoes of the morn ;
And loud the fox-hounds answering bay,
Resounds along the mountain way ;
Whilst harnessed coursers neigh and pace,
Impatient for the coming chase ;
And see, resplendent o'er the world,
The day-god's banner high unfurled.
But all unused the muse to trace,

The tumult of the mountain chase;
More dear to her the peaceful hearth,
Where humble peasants meet in mirth;
Or bid the tear of pity flow,
To way-worn pilgrim's tale of woe,
Who oft the peasant's cheer repays,
With tale of other lands and days.
The cot far up the mountain height;
That housed in peace, our wand'ring wight,
Now hedged around, with winter's snows,
Smiles thro' the beech trees in repose;
No blinding drift and freezing gale
Our youthful hero here assail;
For close beside the hearthstone's blaze,
Beneath its roof he still delays,
And in the cozy fir tree chair,
Receives the kindly matron's care.
My maiden's left at early prime,
The matron spoke, the hill to climb;
Ellen mine own, and only child,
By love of mountain scenes beguiled;
When robed in snow, she deems they stand
Unrivalled in the northern land;
From bold Benevnue, such her boast,
To Ballyhillion's iron coast.
My brother's gentler child our guest,
Reared on a valley's flowry breast,
Where old enchanted Goreymore,
O'er looks Strabreagy's matchless shore;
The champion of her native glens,
For matchless beauty those commends;

Ellen elate with ruder pride,
The issue anxious to decide,
Familiar with each sheltered dell,
Where scarce a snow-wreath ever fell,
Her cousin guides to Craigie Dhu,
Where opes a far extended view,
Hill over hill, and steep on steep,
Where mountain torrents foam and leap,
Now tumbling in the dark ravine,
Now roaring thro' the gorge unseen,
Now hissing o'er a mazy track,
[2]Like that old serpent, huge and black,
Whose bloated bulk and angry mane,
Spread devastation o'er the plain,
Along its track, from Medianmore,
To fair Strabreagy's fartherest shore;
Thus in fond rivalry they strove,
E're starting for the rock above.
Blessed be that love, whose wizard spell,
Gilds barren rock and rugged dell,
With radiant charms—spreads odors rare,
O'er natal scenes, tho' rude and drear;
Could these, my guileless maidens see,
The homes of their proud ancestry,
When the O'Neill, in Kingly power
Bade Faughan shine a regal bower,
Whilst nobles grand, were proud to own
Allegiance to the great Tirown;
How cold to them, how cheerless, drear,
These mountains, and that valley fair.
My mother was a proud O'Neill,

Her sires opposed the English pale:
When sank the star of fair Tirown,
They refuge sought in Inishowen;
There, leagued with gallant Cahir Roe,
Still battled with the ancient foe;
Till charging foremost of the host,
The chieftain fell, then all was lost!
Disaster like a mighty wave,
O'erwhelmned proud chief and clansman biave,
And ruin, like a funeral pall,
In one black level shrouded all;
At times above the dark disguise,
Some scion of our race will rise,
And 'mong the scattered remnants shine;
As fragments of some buried mine,
By earth's couvulsions scattered round,
Tell where the treasures once were found.
Such was my mother! from a child,
No menial toil her cares beguiled;
But such attainments as might grace,
The high-born lady of our race;
She conn'd our glorious records o'er,
And skilled her heart in bardic lore,
Her matchless voice to music wed,
Her fame both far and near was spread;
Till some, the magnates of the land,
Were suitors for her maiden hand;
But earlier love, or ancient pride,
To these the tender boon denied.
An humble suitor gained her grace,
One of Tyrconnel's princely race,

And Hugh O'Donnel won and wed,
The peerless maid of Malinhead.
Such scion was a brother dear,
Who, from his childhood loved to hear
Our mother tell the glorious tales
Of the O'Donnels and O'Neills,
Till swelled his bosom with desires,
All worthy of his honored sires.
Alas, for human hopes, how vain!
His sank, no more to rise again;
The captain of a daring band,
(He loved the sea far more than land,)
Who England's tyrant power defied,
Yet less for lucre, than thro' pride;
When howled the tempest in the night,
And signal rockets rose in sight,
And the slow guns deep solemn boom,
Appall'd the heart, like peal of doom.
Ever these fearless men essayed,
The perilled mariner to aid;
And many a seaman lives to toast,
And bless the men of Malin's coast,
Without whose helping hand to save,
Had long been buried 'neath the wave;
On one such sacred voyage bound,
All, all that noble band were drown'd!
At closing of an autumn day,
A stately ship left Swilly bay;
As set the sun, the land breeze died,
And she, borne by the flooding tide,
The fatal line had nearly cross'd,

Where many a gallant bark was lost;
Whose ruined timbers, black with age,
Defy the Ocean's fiercest rage,
And guard each rock and beech of sand,
From wild Killoort to Polon strand;
Like monuments they stand to tell,
Where fair hopes bade the heart farewell;
That land-locked ship, in her distress,
Showed signal of her helplessness!
Quick, bending to the ready oar,
My brother and his band left shore;
Swift set the current of the tide,
But swifter o'er its breast they glide,
And when upon the deck they stand,
A gallant cheer went up from land!
Ere we could feel the rising gale,
The ship was under easy sail;
With skillful helm, she safe pursued
Her course—where dangerous rocks intrude;
Where many a lofty ship before,
Her canvass furled, to spread no more;
And night, her pitchy banner spread,
Ere they had mastered Malinhead.
Three rockets bursting on the gloom,
And the loud cannon's thund'ring boom,
Sent gladsome tidings from the sea,
And bade us hold high jubilee,
Whilst still we lingered on the strand,
To welcome our returning band.
Now fierce the gale swept from the west,
And lashed to rage the ocean's breast,

Along the beach, the angry swell
Of crested billows, foamed and fell;
Or 'gainst the rocky ramparts beat,
And shook the earth beneath our feet;
Thus ocean's fearful power was moved,
Imperiling those we dearly loved;
Till lips that lately spoke to cheer,
Are pressed in pain, and mute with fear;
Each heart in silent prayer, our friends,
Beyond our aid, to heaven commends;
From out the sea arose a cry,
Of dread, despairing agony:
One answering echo thrill'd the shore,
Then all was silent, as before.
On the next swell that swept the strand,
Their boat was hurled high on the land;
Alas! that gallant, helpless crew,
In that wild cry, bade earth adieu.
Where lonely, Lag sits watching still,
The hallowed grave-yard by the hill;
Sleeping below three mounds of sand,
Lie three of that devoted band;
'Neath wild Killoort's unfriendly wave,
Two kinsmen claim a common grave;
Young Shane O'Neill, the pride and flow'r
Of rude Drumcroy's rocky bower,
And he, my brother, called by men,
Hugh Roe O'Donnel of the Glen.
Oh! had the deep restored our dead,
To rest in consecrated bed,
Where fond affection still could burn,

Its fragrant incense o'er their urn ;
Then sweet the tender tear would flow,
That now, too bitter, drugs our woe.
May He, who earth and sea controls,
Bring peace to their immortal souls,
And comfort those who live to mourn,
The absent, that can ne'er return.
Salt tears suffuse the matron's eyes,
And swelling sobs her speech disguise;
She dried her tears with instant will,
Commands the unbidden sighs be still ;
Those tears I shed, but little grace,
Tyrconnel's haughty, stubborn race ;
She thus resumed, with the O'Neill's,
A softer nature still prevails ;
And to our kin's maternal side,
Are these impulsive throbs allied ;
And so am I, yet fail to trace,
One record in my form or face ;
My mother's son, face form and mind,
In one bright, perfect whole, combined
The rare adornments lost in me,
Of our once proud, ancestral tree ;
And though by death's untimely frost,
Its bloom and glory all are lost,
One gentle offshoot's radiance shines,
And all her father's gifts combines ;
Whilst holiest odors, unconfessed,
To all but Heaven, pervade her breast :
Looks, soul and charms, all harmonize,
And meekly from the world disguise,

The chaste refinements and high art,
That wait, fair handmaids to her heart.
Of her bright gifts most prized by me,
Is song with harp's sweet minstrelsy;
Whether in sorrow's dirge and wail,
Or in the glories of the gael,
Her voice rules like a wizard's wand,
And o'er our hearts holds high command,
Infusing in our souls, the fire,
Or sadness, of the song or lyre;
Her's the same ancient harp that lay,
Neglected, mute and in decay,
[3]Since Daniel of the silver tongue,
With broken heart its chords unstrung;
Condemned the hand would wake its tone,
Till Lords again, of Inishowen,
The rightful heirs of Cahir Roe,
Regained their birth-right from the foe;
And the O'Doherty once more,
Ruled his broad heritage of yore.
A generation passed away,
And still the harp neglected lay;
And still the stranger ruled the land,
And ruled with strong, relentless hand;
Then she of Ulster's ancient kings,
A scion true, restored the strings;
And mistress of the gentle art,
Made captive many a stubborn heart;
And the old glens of Inishowen,
Rejoiced at its inspiring tone.
She strove to train my wayward mind;

To her sweet art I ill inclined;
And startled by my careless stroke,
Discordant, wandering sounds awoke;
And since my mother ceased to sing,
The mold of years lay on the string;
Till our fair songster of the brae,
Renewed its chords to cheer her lay.
Now Celt and Saxon cry, All hail!
To bless the mountain nightingale;
For 'mong the Malin clans her fame,
Is crowned with that sweet songster's name.
Another night, thy rest prolong,
And own the charm of harp and song!
Snow barricades each path and pass,
From Cloghan's bridge, to fair Knockglass;
And ill the luckless trav'ler fares,
Who first the toilsome journey dares.
Those mists, whose airy drap'ry now
Like care o'erspreading beauty's brow,
Slieve Snaght's fair forehead veils from view,
With tears, will soon the vale bedew;
And ere another morning beams,
Dissolve the drift to swell the streams;
Leaving an unobstructed way;
Till then, 'twere better here delay;
And mirth and minstrelsy to-night,
To chase the hours will both unite;
For mountain maids—and swains as free
As maids are fair, hold jubilee;
Whilst Mary, Gorey's flower and pride,
Revives our ancient Christmas tide;

She comes her lonely kin to cheer,
For we are still but strangers here.
Proud England's iron laws, controll'd
By guile, by perjury and gold,
O'erflowed the measure of our ills,
And drove us, exiles to those hills;
From that fair home, a mother's dower,
To him I wed, in Tullaugh's bower.
Five winters' snows have filled the dell,
But my crushed heart may twenty tell,
Since he, on Tullaugh's verdant side,
Despoiled of all, in sorrow died:
Spring, Summer, Autumn reappear,
To crown and guild time's circling year;
But when life's summer-flowers depart,
Unending winter rules the heart;
The broken tendrils clust'ring cling,
But comes to them no vernal spring.
The sorrowing matron left the chair,
To hide the tears upwelling there:
And from the recess, where it lay,
The ancient volume bore away.
Stranger! to while thy tedious time,
Here are our annals, writ in rhyme;
If deeds all noble, proud and high,
Performed in days of chivalry,
Be pleasing task—this lesson learn,
Till back my truant maids return;
They tarry long—the stranger took,
And thanked the matron for the book;
Said, he in distant lands heard tales,

Of the O'Donnels and O'Neills,
From one, whose pride it was to own,
His ancestry from high Tirown ;
For generous heart and martial fire,
The son was worthy of the sire.
Many there are, replied the dame,
In Inishowen, who bear our name;
From Swilly's shore to Malin well,
On hill and glen, our kindred dwell ;
And many a scion, doomed and banned,
Has refuge found in foreign land;
And some, Alas ! That I should say,
Their creed and country both betray !
But our fair deeds recorded there,
In cause of both, will make repair.
Ere yet the youth its clasps withdrew,
A lovelier book attracts his view ;
O'Donnel's daughter, decked in wealth
Of guileless heart, and rosy health,
Came like a sunbeam, soft and warm,
A messenger of light, to charm.
Ah ! gentle stranger, if there be,
In distant land across the sea,
One whose fond heart, like needle true
To magnet—Faithful turns to you,
And thou hast promised, this repay
With faith unfailing, haste away;
If unpremeditated art,
And lay spontaneous sway the heart,
How shall that piiant heart withstand,
The syren-song and conjurer's wand,

When ambushed smile and Erin's lyre,
Against frail flesh and blood conspire ?
Ah ! when did prudent saws prevail,
Where radiant looks like these assail ?
And where is love so fit to die,
As in the light of beauty's eye ?
[4]As dies that bird, whose death illumes,
Its offsprings birth, and guilds its plumes,
And from love's immolating pyre,
Bids love arise, on wings of fire.
The youth with graceful speech commends,
The fond adventure of his friends,
And mourns his dull ungallant sleep ;
Else he had climb'd the mountain keep ;
For with such guides, his toil to share,
The wildest scene, must needs be fair.
Then answered back the blushing maid,
Well may we mourn your absent aid,
Who traced the wintry dells alone,
Thy speech with flowers our path had strown.
The youth replied, that flattery's art,
Was stranger, to his tongue and heart,
And deemed, that others lived, would swear
That wintry landscape past compare,
If two bright fragrant blooms he knew,
Would grace the bower of Creggy Dhu.
Beware ! bold youth, an unknown shore,
Tho' seas be calm, needs dextr'ous oar;
And, oh ! how many a barque there be,
Will fail on love's unfathomed sea :
If such adventure spreads thy sails;

Be thine kind tides and prospering gales,
Yet ! till love's barque in haven fair,
At anchor rests, rash youth, beware !
Why lingers Ellen in the dell ?
The air is chill, what wizard spell,
Can temper rude December's sigh,
With balm of May ? Let youth reply,
And if thou wilt, descend the glade,
Where close she keeps her ambuscade,
Where yon green ivy climbs and clings,
Along the gorge, whilst Cahir sings,
Unconscious of the sweet unrest,
He wakes in Ellen's fluttering breast.

SONG.

I.

Fair is the snow on hill and plain,
  Like her I love, its radiant guise;
And tho' its touch will leave no stain,
  Who woo's its downy pillow dies ;
Yet, fair as wild Glentogher's snows,
  Is my dear maid, and pure as fair;
Blest in the shrine, my hopes repose,
  For love, all warm is watching there.

II.

The blooming rose is queen of June,
  Our summer bower, its fragrance fills ;
And warm its blush, but oh! how soon,
  The autumn blast its beauty chills ;
My Ellen is my bosom's queen,
  Her breath is summer's spicy gales,

Her smile a sunlit ray serene;
  Where blushing love his bliss exhales.

III.

Sweet is the lark's celestial song,
  The linnet's sweet, sweet sings the thrush,
And sweet are all the warbling throng,
  When nature smiles, that now are hush;
Still sweeter love's melodious sighs,
  Awake my bosom's deeper swell;
When tears bedew my Ellen's eyes,
  For love lies mirrored in the well.

IV.

In vain have richer lovers tried,
  With softer speech to wile the flower,
That blooms on rude Glentogher's side,
  To softer vale, and chaster bower.
Our rugged mountain's solitude,
  My Ellen loves, tho' wild it be;
And tho' by harsher accents woo'd,
  The rose still blooms for love and me.

Thus sang the youthful mountaineer,
And poured his soul on Ellen's ear;
Deeming the tender ditty fell,
On callous Crag—and icy dell;
And Ellen when she clim'd the glade,
Had no design of ambuscade,
Nor dreamt her lover's care would guide
His footsteps up Glentogher's side.
The wintry tempest's sudden war,

Spread his bewildered flocks afar,
In scattered clusters, where its shock
Was broken by some friendly rock;
Besieged by snow, without his care,
The hungry fold would perish there.
A mile below the ivied ridge,
The cloghan pathway seeks the bridge,
Now of the arch, the only trace,
One flanking wall, one ruined base.
The shepherd thus impelled per force,
Must trace the torrent's higher course;
Along its bank the pathway led,
Where granite boulders crossed its bed;
Rude stepping stones, where daring men
In deadly peril gain the glen;
The youth a passage here essayed,
Then turned him down the softer glade;
Where to the right, a space above
He deemed yon cottage held his love,
Such warm desires his bosom throng,
As woke his heart's spontaneous song;
Sweet stole the words to Ellen's ear,
As those sweet sounds, the sainted hear,
When pleading love, removes the bar,
And leaves the heavenly gates ajar;
If doubt, or fear e'er crossed her heart,
The generous lay bade all depart,
And joy, love, hope and faith allied,
And oh! forgive that throb of pride;
With the wild rush the rebel came,
An instant more, a holier flame

Explored the chambers of her breast;
And spurned the rude unbidden guest.
The maid had gained a lofty dell,
When on her ear the music fell,
Where bright immortal ivy spread
Its wintry foliage o'er her head,
Whilst giant fern around her grew,
And hid her slender form from view.
Yet, like some terror stricken deer,
Low on the ground she nestled here.
The mountain ash, its autumn yield
Of burnished clusters, here revealed ;
And bending to the maiden's hand,
Its treasures lay at her command,
Ere Cahir's footsteps gained the wall,
In fright her berries she let fall.
These, on her lovers path below,
Like beads of coral decked the snow :
Lay garnered too, the path beside
The holly boughs for Christmas tide,
All tell-tale emblems well designed,
To court the gaze, but love is blind ;
And busy with his tender lay,
The youth, unheeding kept his way.
Had pearls of price, lay scattered round,
Not one that ardent youth had found;
One pearl within his breast enshrined
Alone, was present to his mind ;
Oh ! had he scan'd the russet fern,
He might a peerless gem discern,
Whose ray's soft radiance bathed in dew

Those dark fringed lashes veil'd from view ;
Methinks, he then had made delay,
Nor thus so quickly sped away.
Soon as his form was lost to ken,
The maiden issued from the glen ;
The green-wood boughs she quickly bound,
But left her berries scattered round ;
Fled up the hill, like hunted doe,
Nor turned around to gaze below ;
The holly folded in her arms,
The cottage closed around her charms.
'Twere well the maiden looked not back,
For following close her fleeing track,
A form of long and lusty stride,
Pressed boldly up the mountain's side ;
A seal-skin cap his temples graced,
A rapier belted to his waist ;
The burden on his shoulders bound,
Might weigh a pack-horse to the ground ;
Where cups and cans, and varied gear,
And garniture of war, appear ;
And as his sturdy bulk he flung,
The hill to climb, they clanke'd and rung ;
His leggings buckled to the knee,
So tight below, the eye could see
The sinews play, whilst limb and stride,
Showed iron strength to grace allied ;
Without alarm the porch he passed,
And graced the floor, the maids aghast !
Beheld his stern, yea, savage gaze,
And trembling, shunned the piercing rays ;

From o'er his brow his cap he drew,
And full exposed his face to view;
Frowned that bold frontlet, black and high,
As cloud, when thunder rends the sky;
A girdling ring like iron band,
In circle black, his temples spann'd;
And gave the swarthy face below,
A fiery, fierce, forbidding glow;
His shaggy beard stood torn and shred,
Like heather tufts on mountain's head,
When moorland fires have swept the hill,
Yet left unscathed a remnant still;
Whilst o'er the whole his eye of pride,
Each gazer's timid look defied.
Pardon, he said, a pilgrim rude,
Whose wanderings on your home intrude;
The torrent from the mountain ridge,
Has swept away the Cloghan's bridge;
The ancient footpath I explored,
That crosses at the gulley's ford;
And thus to reach my native vale,
The mountain's toilsome way I scale:
I crossed it once, but years ago,
'Twas unobstructed then with snow.
Crossed with a blithsome merry throng,
Who smoothed the road with jest and song.
McColgan in this homestead then
Kept bed and board for foot sore men;
And I, by that same hope betrayed,
In search of rest, your peace invade:
Deeming the "House upon the hill,"

Its comforts spreads for travelers still.
Yet thou canst show, and I thy grace
Will thank—the nearest resting place;
He paused to hear, prepared to go,
The matron answered, Stranger, no!
Whilst Irish homes hold Irish hearts,
No friend nor enemy departs;
If hungered, till he share our cheer,
If weary, rest—then rest thee here.
Glentogher's crest is hard to scale,
And still beyond lies marshy vale;
And farther yet, against the skies,
The heights of Glenagannon rise,
And on a dreary moor look down,
Where Herald keeps the "Harp and Crown."
The track that leads across the waste,
Is now by drifted snow effaced,
And with the rains that lately fell,
The ford is flooded in the dell.
That moorland path is seldom trod,
In summer, save by foot outlawed;
To weary stranger failing here,
'Tis filled with peril, toil and fear.
On yonder cushion seek such rest,
As woo's a foot sore weary guest;
What else thy needful wants require,
Is thine to show. Nought I desire,
But freedom from this lumber pack,
That weighs and chafes my yielding back;
And place a while to lay my head.
My pillow this; a downy bed

Ill suits a rugged soldier's mood;
The rougher settle, mates the rude,
Were it of granite harsh and cold,
The words of welcome you unfold,
Would make its hard unyielding breast,
To grateful heart a couch of rest.
At once his knapsack he unslung,
And on the floor beside him flung;
One blanket on the bench he spread,
And one he folded for his head;
Removed his belt, but placed the brand,
Where he could reach it with his hand;
Precaution thus, 'gainst sudden strife,
Seems instinct in a soldier's life;
Without another word essayed,
Full on the bench his form he laid;
A moment round the circle gazed,
Then to the roof his vision raised;
Above his brow, as if to shield
From view, the sternness there revealed,
His arms he crossed, then mute and blind
To thoughts of home his soul resigned.
'Twere wrong to say the matron's breast,
Took kindly to her moody guest;
When first his visage she beheld,
His looks, her troubled soul repelled;
And fear alone, forbade her fly,
The lightnings of his roving eye;
His black and battered visage told,
Of desperate strife, and struggle bold;
Perhaps, in honor's bright career,

Perhaps, as ruthless buccaneer ;
Such dread misgivings took control,
And for a space oppressed her soul;
Yet not for this would she deny,
The rights of hospitality.
Then something in his voice's tone,
Bade her each darker thought disown.
So to these tender maidens here,
He came a harbinger of fear.
And still his form in rest reclin'd,
With awe o'erpowers each timid mind.
The youth alone his joy confessed,
As he surveyed the sullen guest ;
At times, his prostrate form he eyed,
With kindling smile and glance of pride ;
At times, his gaze regret betrayed ;
That he, unsocial, thus delayed ;
Awhile a cold and gloomy spell,
On that fair circle frowned and fell ;
And when they spoke, 'twas with such breath,
As curbs our voice in house of death!
They spoke of holy Christmas near,
And of its blithe and blessed cheer ;
Spoke of that love whose depths beguil'd,
To Bethlehem's stall, the wond'rous child,
Spoke of the high celestial strains,
By shepherd's heard on Judahs plains,
" Glory to God in highest heaven ;
And peace on earth to men forgiven,"
Thro' holy faith each vision strays,
And owns that star's mysterious rays,

That bade the Magi, seek the shrine,
Where Mary watched the babe divine ;
'Till they, like those their gifts unfold,
Of myrrh, of frankinsence and gold,
And bend adoring heart and knee,
Before a God's humility.
They spoke of Mary's wond'rous bliss,
Whose lips immaculate may kiss
Incarnate God ! who veils his charms,
And glory in his mother's arms !
Oh ! Royal babe bring thou to me
The fruits of thy nativity.
Oh ! Virgin Mother undefiled,
Look down on me a wayward child,
With watchful care and smile benign,
As on that happy circle shine ;
Who on Glentogher's rugged side,
Now weave green boughs for Christmas tide,
And thus in holy converse blest,
They grew oblivious of their guest,
And mirth resumed her smiling reign,
Till frightened from her throne again,
By sudden sob, as if the heart,
That gave it birth, had split apart.
All eyes the stranger's couch invade,
No change the prostrate man betrayed,
Except that quicker rose and fell,
His mighty bosom's living swell,
Like ocean wave that breaks its force,
On wreck, and sinks in middle course.
Comrade ! as if the word could charm,

The soldier raised upon his arm,
And ere the youth his tale confessed,
Those eyes of fire his speech arrest;
Like meteor bursting on the night,
When skies are calm, so flashed the light,
Swift, fierce and silent, like that ray,
As swift and silent passed away;
And back upon his rugged bed,
Again he laid his shaggy head.
Soldier! the youth once more began,
Thou seem'st a weary, way-worn man;
Thy garb and bearing both betray,
Thou'st seen rough usage in thy day.
Comrade! I lay no stronger claim,
To use that free, familiar name;
Than one like thee, by winds adverse,
Was driven from his destined course;
And yesterday, was glad to moor,
Where you, to-day, your barque secure;
And still by our good dame's request,
I linger here, a willing guest;
For who would hurry hence away,
Tho' it were summer's balmiest day,
From haven fair, where beauty's smile,
And angel hands our cares beguile;
The glorious sun's effulgence bright,
The wintry landscape bathes in light;
Why waste the golden hours of prime,
In solitude's unsocial clime?
Whilst day-light dreams, you know, at best,
Are harbingers of night's unrest.

'Tis churlish! here's a vacant chair;
Draw near, and chase unhealthy care,
With merry song or roundelay,
Of love, or war, or grave or gay;
Or, if it better suit your mood,
Be early chilhood's scenes renewed;
Or, give our gentle household here,
Some tidings of thy rough career,
Thy haps, and 'scapes by land and sea,
Pains, penalties and jeopardy!
For me, for thee, I'm bound to say,
Our freinds are keeping holiday;
And who so gen'rous with his store,
When asked to pay an honest score,
As soldier, gallant, bold and free,
Then comrade, seek our company.
At once, the soldier raised his head,
And turning, left his rugged bed;
A moment glanced on all around,
Then knelt him on the naked ground;
His hands together gently closed,
Upon his ample chest reposed,
His eyes half shrouded of their blaze,
High on the roof-tree fixed their gaze;
His lips moved busily in prayer,
But not a sound the list'ners share;
Then humbling low his lofty crest,
His forehead on the floor he pressed;
Then signed the cross upon his breast.
A minute scarcely passed away,
Since that rude soldier knelt to pray;

Eternity may yet reveal,
That fervent silent brief appeal.
And now erect upon his feet,
He seek's and fills the vacant seat;
I own my churlish mood to-day,
Doth thy kind welcome ill repay;
But memories sweet and sad arise,
If I a moment veil my eyes;
As I approach my native vale,
Warm hopes awake, fresh fears assail,
Oh! who may say, but he of lies,
The father, comes in such disguise,
To wound the soul with poisoned barb;
Decked in affections holiest garb.
Or, why should I my heart beguiled,
By memories tender, sweet and wild;
Of home, of wife, of children fair,
Forget our lady's noon day prayer?
That prayer, that by my mother's knee,
Her sainted lips revealed to me,
That prayer since then my lips have told,
As morning, noon and night unrolled.
At times when deadly shot and shell,
Fierce, on our reeling columns fell,
Striking our bravest on the plain,
As reapers autumn's ripened grain.
And swept by wars unpitying tide,
In gory heaps—to kneel denied,
I've stood mid carnage and despair,
And silent owned our Lady's prayer.
And in the camp 'mong comrades rude,

Loud laugh and ridicule withstood;
The ruffian jest, the bigot's sneer,
Defied them all, to falter here;
Here, where no mocking tongues invade,
Thro' selfish love thy cause betrayed.
And, Oh! how many an evil hour,
My mistress mild, my mystic flower;
My tender, chaste, maternal Dove,
I've passed, unscathed—Thy wings above,
Then help, bright, gentle Queen, I pray,
Thy recreant child, again to day;
Each idol of my heart dethrone,
And rule high sovereign Queen—alone;
Whilst these shall learn, and I declare,
Thy generous aid, in my despair;
In that dread hour of my career,
When sank my sonl, the slave of fear.

THE SOLDIER'S TALE.

It happened once upon a day,
Whilst near the foe our forces lay;
I disobeyed some slight command,
Of one who ruled with iron hand,
As captain of our rugged band;
In presence of our whole brigade,
Who, for field exercise arrayed,
Were witness of the dark disgrace,
He rudely struck me on the face;
I would have stabbed him in the breast,
But ready hands my aim arrest;
And me disarm· Then with a curse,

I sprung, and dragged him off his horse;
O'erpowered at once and borne away,
Was tried and sentenced that same day;
Short was the shrift, and sure the ban,
'Twas thus the martial finding ran;
" To-morrow, on the self-same spot
And hour, the culprit will be shot;
But first, for disobedience flog,
With thirty stripes, then shoot the dog!"
Now was my heart of hope debarred,
In durance watched by double guard,
And manacled, as sad I lay,
Within my cell, at close of day;
In solitude, whilst queries dread,
Before my anguished soul were spread,
Where wilt thou, ere another night,
Oh! stubborn soul have winged thy flight?
Will hell rejoice, and angels weep,
And horrors haunt eternal sleep?
Or, Seraphs spread their glowing wings,
To waft thee to the King of Kings?
Where ransomed souls forever more,
Around the throne, their God adore;
Oh! wretched soul so soon to go,
To break that seal of bliss or woe,
In God's great book of death or life.
Ah! little thought I then of wife,
Of children dear, of home, of all;
The human heart can hold in thrall,
My sins, both sense and soul appall,
Legion on legion they arise,

Monsters in every shape and guise;
I wept, put every burning tear,
That wet my hands, did blood appear.
I tried to pray, but furies foul,
.Mocked my despairing words with howl;
Hope shrank dismayed, whilst vampires spread
Their horrid pinions o'er my head;
I deemd there talons clutched my hair,
Oh! dreadful sin of sad despair;
Thank heaven, I live, that sin to tell,
And stigmatize—the bugles swell
In cadence soft serene and clear,
Broke on my dream of guilt and fear,
And grace triumphant o'er despair,
Awoke once more my vesper prayer:
Then hope resumed her heav'nly sway;
And Mary's smiles my fears allay.
Ere half my orisons were o'er,
Beneath my prisons oaken floor,
Where on my humbled forehead pressed,
A shock and jar, my thoughts arrest,
A square, perhaps two feet or so,
Of solid plank went down below;
A packet fell upon the floor,
And instant closed the secret door.
The purport instantly I guessed,
I hid the parcel in my breast,
'Till with my hands, tho' shackled still,
I gathered dust, the joints to fill.
And all was ready, when the guard,
The entrance to my cell unbarr'd.

A soldier burly, rude and free,
Was Hugh O'Donnel of Ardee;
Comrade ! he said, and namesake too,
A suppliant, I your pardon sue,
My faults I own and all arraign,
Each reckless jest that caused you pain;
Forget harsh words too often spoke,
Forbear ! the vengence these awoke,
Forgive what else I have done amiss,
He raised my shackled hands to kiss,
His face he buried in my hands,
Till tears be-dewed the iron bands;
Big sobs his manly bosom swell,
And whilst he closed the dreary cell,
He cried ! O'Donnel, fare-thee-well.
Hold ! comrade, broke the youthful guest,
No need of secret manifest;
No pirate craft, no privateer,
Embargo or blockade is here,
Hoist your true flag, the coast is clear.
What speech is this, presumptuous boy?
That I use guile and base decoy,
If such the purport it denote,
I thrust the falsehood down your throat.
He rudely pushed him from his seat,
The supple youth sprung on his feet,
As if prepared for bloodly work,
From hidden scabdard drew a dirk,
Cried ! murder blazing in his eyes,
Now, Black O'Neill I tear thy guise.
Like panther springing from his lair,

Swift sprung the soldier from his chair,
Grasped in his iron clutch the brand,
And wrenched it from the stripling's hand,
As Tennis player checks the ball,
Pitched his assailant to the wall;
Above his head the weapon flung,
Roof-tree and rafters shivering rung;
Where from the reach of all debarred,
The steel, stuck buried to the guard;
Backed where his garniture was stored,
And caught at once his ready sword;
Drew from the sheath the shining blade,
With glance of fire the scene surveyed,
Then glaring like some beast of prey,
Within its den, he stood at bay.
That rash attack with deadly knife,
Insulting word, and instant strife,
So sudden came, so quickly passed,
Each gentle maiden stood aghast,
With sense confounded, heart appalled;
And loud on heaven for succor called.
The matron silent and amazed;
On that fierce face intently gazed,
Then dropping on her knees implored,
With lifted hands, Put down thy sword;
Oh! Christian man with Christian gore,
Drench not our lowly cabin's floor;
For Christ's dear sake do not besmear,
Thy ransomed soul with murder here.
Murder or shedding human blood,
The soldier cried, if such my mood,

Or my intent, his naked brand,
And breast were both at my command;
In self-defence, I keep my guard,
For treacherous friend and foe prepared;
And only hold my sheathless blade,
To foil foul blow and ambuscade;
And see my faithful handmaids nigh,
With lamps well trimmed, their tapers dry;
He held a brace of pistols high,
Then on his rival fixed his eye,
With searching look, rash boy thy tale
Declare—where met thee Black O'Neill.
But hold! first let us make amends,
To these, our hospitable friends;
Mother! arise, forgive the need,
Of mine array for hostile deed;
Trained in the camp, the soldier's ear,
From harmless sounds wins notes of fear;
But sure no hostile band is here;
And you, my children, gentle, fair,
So help me Heaven, whilst I declare,
I'd rather hazard mortal harm,
Than give your innocence alarm;
My visage scarred, and blackened brow,
May frighten timid maidens now;
'Mid maddening scenes, on many a field,
This arm did aye the helpless shield;
And never dealt to open foe,
Or treacherous friend, unmanly blow.
Comrade! our hasty broil forget,
And show where you and I have met;

If e'er before. The youth replied,
'Twas on the transport Queen of Clyde;
The winds asleep, the waves at rest,
Becalmed upon the ocean's breast;
One bugle's pensive notes arose,
All harsher sounds had sought repose;
Then instant tumult spoke aloud,
And swayed and surged a madden'd crowd;
A score of men would one assail,
With cries of death to black O'Neill;
Then first I saw thee, saw thy foes,
A wall of steel around thee close;
Watched thy red hand and shining blade,
And thee, undaunted, undismayed;
With giant force and iron will,
Beat back thy fierce assailers still!
I saw you when your sabre broke,
And staggered by the erring stroke,
Full on the slippery deck you fell,
Your foemen closing with a yell,
Like bloodhounds; then I saw you throw
The hilt, against the foremost foe,
And as he reeled beneath the blow,
Ere he could raise his drooping sword,
You, with your prey, went overboard.
Now, black O'Neill, say if I lie,
Or, of my answer ought deny.
The soldier cried, that will not I;
By your ill mannered name I own,
Among those ruffians I was known;
Yet still me thinks you could relate,

What might my quarrel vindicate ;
I own, you told the story well,
And wish you now the sequel tell;
What pains and penalties were mine,
For breach of martial discipline,
And risk of life—full well you know,
A life was periled in each blow ;
'Till broke my brand. If what I said,
Has these, our witnesses misled,
Or prejudiced your cause, I swear,
All owned thy courage high and rare ;
Thy cause unknown, then let me trace
That glorious final act of grace,
That wedded hero to thy name,
With twice two hundred men's acclaim,
Loud rung thy foes exulting yell ;
When on the deck, unarmed you fell ;
But when on Wilson Grey you sprung,
And hoarse with rage this challange flung :
Now Wilson Grey, or you, or I,
Or both, this day are doomed to die;
Whilst headlong o'er the vessel's rail,
You and your rival pitched—O'Neill;
Then rose such cry upon the air,
Of disappointment, rage, despair,
As fiends might raise when seraphs bright,
Throw round a soul, a shield of light,
And bear to mercy's radiant throne,
The rescued one they deemed their ow n.
Before that howl of horror died,
The bugles brazen voice replied ;

To arms ! to arms ! each martial band,
At once obeyed the stern command ;
Whilst I, beheld with awe below,
Amid the wave, each struggling foe.
Like mighty monsters of the deep,
Who mid its depths their gambols keep ;
Up from the ocean's depth arose,
In locked embrace those panting foes ;
Now arms extended at full length,
Yet grappling still with all their strength;
Each strives, with varying success,
Beneath the wave his foe to press.
Thrice closed the waters o'er their strife,
And thrice they rose to gasp for life ;
And thrice upon the ocean's breast,
They lay apart, awhile to rest ;
And now, as near again they drew,
The deadly struggle to renew ;
Grey's courage with his strength did fail,
Save me, he cried, I drown, O'Neill !
His arms the waves at random smote,
The salt spray gurgling in his throat.
Mysterious man ! then were fulfilled,
Thy plight of vengeance, had thou will'd ;
But in this cry of dire distress,
Thy conquered comrade's helplessness,
Yielding to mercy's high command,
You lent your foe a helping hand ;
And held him, like a child, afloat,
Till reached and rescued by a boat ;
Then rose a long and lusty cheer,

From many a gallant witness here;
Who in the rigging's dizzy height,
Intently watched the desperate fight.
Again it rises, high and higher,
Instant as magazine on fire;
O'er all the ship, above, below,
Sailor and soldier, friend and foe,
Unite in one harmonious cheer,
Long live the gallant grenadier!
The fife's shrill notes and rattling drums,
Struck, "See the conquering hero comes,"
When on the quarter deck you stood,
All dripping from the briny flood.
Well may I deem thy natal hour,
Was ruled by some propitious power;
Whose geni wards and watches still,
Thy foe to foil, or work thy will;
Else I, a sterner tale could tell
Than this, that strangely ended well.
That morn, that saw our ship set sail,
To woo the ocean's fresh'ning gale;
Whilst yet at anchor in the bay,
A barge close by our vessel lay;
A soldier, feeble, wan and worn,
Was from the barge by seamen borne.
His rank was high, and fair his fame,
'Till fortune, faithless, fickle dame,
Alone in view of his command,
Betrayed him to a hostile band;
In durance close, and long confined
With fractured limb, his fervid mind

Brooding with sorrow and remorse;
O'er fame's eclipse and errant course,
His soul had nearly win his way,
From prison to eternal day:
And now a ruin stately drear,
Alone remained of brave St Clair;
Few saw him to his cabin borne,
And none beheld him since that morn,
Save him who ruled the martial band,
His next Lieutenant in command,
And one a citizen, whose care,
In prison soothed his pain's despair,
Now his companion guest or groom,
None other entered in his room;
On that same day, that very hour,
When nature husbanding her power,
Left our good ship a lazy mass,
Scarce moving on that sea of glass;
Saint Clair, now somewhat stronger grown,
Was pacing on the deck alone;
Slow was his step, as one who tried,
Some feat of hazard, long denied.
His ever present friend stood near,
And poured upon his raptured ear,
The martial bugle's tender swell,
Where music's soul delights to dwell.
Then fearful clamor woke fierce cry,
Dethroning music's pensive sigh;
Then blazed St Clair, thine eye of fire,
And swelled thy throbbing breast with ire;
But when that yell of fierce despair,

From foiled assailants rent the air;
He grasped the bugle's brazen throat,
And blew in rage the battle-note;
That note, which to the soldier's ear,
Of conflict tells, of pain and fear,
And death. If faithless to his band,
He falter at the stern command;
When on St. Clair, my gaze I turned,
His eyes, like glowing fagots burned;
His aid—in fearful wrath he spurned,
Ah! then, O'Neill, thy fate I mourned.
Ho, monster! cried the frantic chief,
Or fiend! which art thou? speak, be brief.
He raised his arm, his brow to guard,
As if his soul the sight abhorred;
Instant you bounded on the deck,
To where he stood, a shattered wreck;
You roared—Perfideous, base St. Clair!
Behold your black hand-writing there;
Your finger on your temples pressed,
Then snatching something from your breast;
This pledge dishonored—like a coal,
It brands and burns my very soul;
I spurn thy gift, and perfidy—
And both despise. Now, God on high
Be witness! thus, St. Clair began,
I own I wronged thee wretched man,
And wrought thee harm; but broken plight,
Or ought would stain an honored knight,
Or his escutcheon blur or blot,
Or stigmatize—upbraid me not:

I give thee welcome with my hand,
And own, before my shattered band,
In gen'rous act, and courage rare,
No peer hast thou. That I, St. Clair,
With word of gall, and hasty blow,
Unmerited ; made thee my foe ;
Till fortune in her fitful hour,
Left me, all helpless, in thy power ;
Uprose thy soul, triumphant still,
And rendered good for deed of ill ;
And in that deed heroic, spread
Those living coals around my head ;
Whose glowing flames, and sacred fire,
Will last, till love and life, expire ;
That life you periled all to shield,
This love, alas ! too late reveal'd.
St. Clair's embrace his love express'd,
O'Neill, alone, can tell the rest.
Ere yet I close, I own my fault,
Regret my reckless, rude assault ;
And all amend, you may desire,
I render, for the deed of ire ;
My life within your conquering power
Preserved, I grateful hold the dower ;
Long as will flow the crimson tide—
Comrade, enough the soldier cried,
The open speech has seldom plan'd,
Foul strategy, the hasty hand;
Tho' oft it work a deed of harm
It can't undo, speaks bosom warm ;
Long may that gen'rous current run,

'Til tempered by thy ev'ning sun,
Its final ebb and last repose,
May virtue's golden sands disclose.
We still are friends; this maiden sword
I give, as hostage, for my word;
The legend graven on its blade,
When I my tale have told, may aid,
To read the riddle why I claim,
Then black O'Neill another name.
He drew the scabbard o'er the brand,
And placed them in the stripling's hand,
Whilst peace above that little world,
Once more her banner has unfurled;
And confidence revived, restored,
Seats all around the social board,
The soldier, thus unites again,
His story's rudely broken chain.
I stood unmoved until the guard,
The prison portal closed and barred;
Then gnawed the cord the packet tied,
And found a shackle's key inside;
Each minute seemed an hour to me,
'Till I had worked my right hand free;
I left in strategy the band,
Encircling still the other hand;
Then stealthy as a cat, I stole
Close to the narrow window hole,
Where twilight struggling thro' the grate,
Helped me to read the book of fate.
Hope—thus the missive read—and keep
Thy ears on guard—beware of sleep;

When quarrel loud and drunken strife,
Disturb your guard, then work for life;
One foot pushed heavy on the door,
Will force the passage thro' the floor,
Descend, nor fear the gloomy vault;
Secure the trap with iron bolt,
Lay hold the rope, pull with your mig ht,
And trust to God your future flight;
If in the swamp you be delayed,
To-morrow may bring further aid;
Destroy this record, friends are few,
But tried and faithful all—Adieu.
Oh! what mysterious powers control,
And rule and warp the heart and soul;
A moment past when dread remorse,
Portrayed my sins, and sinful course;
I'd barter life without a sigh,
For one to teach me how to die;
Tho' most unworthy priestly hand,
Of all our holy churches band;
And now my wayward changeful breast,
Owns love of life its fondest guest;
I dropped at once upon the floor,
The secret trap to find once more.
Slow as a snail, the journey made,
'Til on the door my cheek I laid;
I tore the note to shun mishap,
And eat the paper, scrap by scrap;
Then stretched me down within the cell,
But all my soul stood sentinel.
The soldier paused, as if to train

The wandering memories of the brain ;
And thus his tale resumed again :
Perhaps 'twere better here to say,
Our camping ground in former day,
Had been a haven of resort,
For men with iron souls ; a port
Where pirate craft, and pirate crew,
Could safe their hellish trade pursue ;
And Christ's redeemed of sable dye,
Like beasts of burden sell and buy ;
But war with retributive hand,
The robbers slew, the traffic banned,
And mart, and hamlet, where we lay,
Were sunk to ruin and decay.
The village crowned a gentle hill,
And in the valley sat the mill ;
A structure, solid, broad, and bold,
That must have cost a mine of gold ;
The architect the building planned,
Part in the sea, and part on land ;
And with his skill its power supplied,
From endless ebb and flow of tide ;
But now by brambles overgrown,
Lay buried deep its arch of stone,
And long canal. A reckless few,
The boldest of our rugged crew,
That gloomy passage had explored,
And in its bowels plunder stored.
One end was open to the sea,
The other choked by bush and tree ;
And hidden in a trackless waste,

Its opening could not now be traced.
The mill contained five hundred men,
Yet of them all, but only ten
Had knowledge of the mystic way,
That 'neath my cell and pillow lay;
Those ten, a sworn and secret band,
Had for this night carousal planned;
And from below such stores conveyed,
As oft their midnight revels made.
And of these ten, the boldest three,
Brave Hugh O'Donnel, of Ardee,
Fierce Cameron, of the Isle of Skie,
And one, Sir Arthur's orderly,
A comrade from my native vale,
Peace to your ashes, true O'Neill!
Held council how to rescue me,
And from my peril set me free;
The rest gave good and timely aid,
Unconscious of the part they played;
And as I learned in after day,
From Hugh O'Donnel, this the way:
O'Neill, the master mind and guide,
Tho' seldom from his master's side,
To each his needed part supplied;
O'Donnel sought the secret door,
And flung the packet on the floor,
And had himself detailed for guard,
For what would follow, well prepared;
Whilst Duncan Cameron plied his art,
In working up each comrade's heart,
For lawless act—to seek my cell,

O'er awe a d bind the sentinel,
Then drag me out from where I lay,
And hang me, ere the break of day.
O'Donnel's parting loud good night,
Was signal plann'd, that all was right.
Two tedious hours had passed, when lo!
A soldier staggering to and fro,
Approached the guard, then reeling fell,
Close to the entrance of the cell;
Another, and another came,
And some the guard began to blame;
When one, a boaster at the best,
Their purpose openly expressed;
O'Donnel placed him in arrest.
Ill did his comrades brook the thrall,
And then began such drunken brawl,
As swelled with strife the rising gale,
And reached Sir Arthur and O'Neill,
For with his orderly as aid,
The midnight camp he oft surveyed;
And woe betide the luckless guard,
Who at his post was unprepared;
Of their mad purpose being told,
Their zeal, Sir Arthur now controlled;
Called for a light and sought the cell,
And as he entered, gave a yell;
The fiend has fled, call out the guard,
And every pass and passage ward.
Full fifty men that instant found,
From mote to mote the mill surround;
The drunken boaster, fain to show

His hatred of his captains's foe,
Cried out! Sir Arthur, follow me,
We'll catch him ere he gets to sea;
I know the secret outlet well;
It opens in the ruffian's cell.
Half drunk with rum, with fury blind,
He left Sir Arthur far behind,
And gained the outlet of the moat,
As ushered forth my flimsy boat;
He raised a rock to crush the raft,
And loud the drunken ruffian laughed;
Then reeling missed his evil aim,
And headlong tumbled in the stream;
The pitchy wave closed o'er his head,
Bedaubed with filth, with rapine red,
His soul—all rank to judgment fled.
The matron groaned in agony,
Prepare us, Lord, in peace to die;
And thrice, on brow, on lips and breast,
Salvation's sacred sign impressed.
I stooped to gain a better view,
The narrow channel to pursue;
And in the dark my wandering hand,
Regained, and clutched the shackle's band
I flung the iron at my foe,
Sir Arthur just escaped the blow;
It grazed in flight his stooping crest,
And struck O'Neill upon the breast;
I saw him stagger on the strand,
And grasp his master's helping hand;
Ere others came to bar the way,

My boat had gained a broader bay;
And ere my labor, I forbore,
I must have gained a mile from shore;
Alone—'mid solitude profound,
And darkness drear; but whither bound?
This query in my mind expressed,
I laid aside my oar to rest,
And on my knees I crept with care,
To know the most my craft would bear
Of rougher hazard—but as well,
To risk me in a cockle shell;
I, in this search discovered store
Of rations, for a week or more;
With two canteens, my throat was dry,
I drew the cork, the first to try;
I spurned the liquid from my mouth,
Tho' I was pained, and parched with drouth;
The other held that gift of heaven,
So much desired, so freely given;
The sweet libation flowed amain,
My thirst its deepest drop would drain;
I saved a part, lest worse betide,
And slung the vessel by my side;
And of my future course and fate,
Within my mind did thus debate:
My raft unseaworthy and frail,
Will founder in the slightest gale,
And even if I get to sea,
'Twere but to meet the foe I flee,
For England's floating bulwarks lay,
Like bull dogs, watching port and bay;

For miles, yea many leagues around,
Morass and trackless wastes abound;
A sea, at highest flood of tide,
I prayed to Heaven my course to guide.
A rocket rising in the air,
Lit up the scene with sudden glare;
That secret signal's firey trail,
Did oft before my watch assail,
And fixed my purpose, weal or woe,
I'll seek proud England's haughty foe.
The doom of death without appeal,
Recorded by a hand of steel,
Could in my desp'rate peril plead,
And of dishonor purge the deed.
But I had higher, holier cause,
In England's violated laws,
For from my native Island sea,
I had been torn by perfidy,
The victim of a nation's crime,
Was forced away to foreign clime;
Beneath far India's burning skies,
My visage gained its swarthy guise,
For two long years of toil and care,
Mid war and plagues, I wasted there.
Thence to the Western world afar,
Placed foremost in the ranks of war;
On many a field of blood I strove
To crush the liberty I love,
But ravage, rapine, ruin failed,
And war's red lightning's waned and paled,
As rose that constellation grand,

In triumph o'er the rescued land.
And lost to England's diadem,
Forever lost that priceless gem;
Another signal rocket's ray,
Again reveals my destined way,
My shallop jumps at every stroke,
'Till sad mishap my paddle broke;
The longer portion in the sea,
Whilst scarce a foot remained with me.
I judged as best I might, the wind,
Now blowing fresh, was dead behind,
And in the locker of the boat,
Around my rations lay a coat,
A spacious garment, faded brown,
Had been Sir Arthur's dressing gown;
I learned its purpose at a guess,
'Twas left to screen my gaudy dress,
With hat of felt—they both had made,
The Quaker of our masquerade.
That hat, my forage cap replaced;
I donned the dressing gown in haste,
Then standing on the forward rail,
My self for mast, my gown the sail,
Its generous folds my arms outspread,
My little shallop shot ahead
In splendid style, an hour or more;
At last a bramble caught her prore,
And round she swung her stern ashore;
Above my head in deepest gloom,
My hand could feel the mosses' plume,
Whilst reaching thus my way to trace,

A bat in flight assailed my face,
I struck the monster with my hand,
But of my foot-hold lost command,
Then grasped by chance a vine that hung
Within my reach, and instant sprung;
My boat, the sudden impulse sent,
Back to her native element ;
And I, 'mid darkness and despair,
Like felon struggling in the air :
I almost failed to force a pass,
So closely twined the tangled mass,
And when I gained the upper air,
I laid me down, exhausted there.
The centre yielding to my weight,
Declined a space, the sides elate,
Like canopy enclosed my bed;
The sea breeze whistling o'er my head,
In fitful gusts blew harmless by.
And sung a mournful lullaby ;
A grateful feeling of repose,
Like balm o'er all my being flows ;
I strove a suppliant prayer to say,
But sleep my senses stole away,
And dreams of bliss, and visions fair,
Did to my couch with sleep repair.

END OF SECOND CANTO.

THE FRIAR'S CURSE—CANTO THIRD.

Who has not—In the circle of long years,
  Amid life's stubborn trials that confound
His youthful hopes—wringing the bitter tears
  From anguished heart: When sleep his senses bound
Owned bliss ecstatic, all his soul surround
  In dreams of early love, or brighter prize
Of Hymen's crown of Myrtle. Such, if found,
  May cavil at the tear drops that disguise
That battered face of bronze, and glisten in his eyes.
    The soldier stayed awhile his tale,
    And with his iron hand would veil
    The tears, that struggling through the night,
    Of that dark visage, shine more bright,
    As diamonds sparkle most, when set
    In coronal or crown of jet;
    But quick he dried the limpid stain,
    And thus connects his story's chain:

THE SOLDIER'S TALE—(Continued.)

The charmer of my boyhood's years,
Chaste in her matron pride appears;
Mild as the balmy breath of May,

9*

And radiant as the rainbow's ray.
We wandered by the lakelet's strand,
With our two darlings hand in hand;
The sea was calm, the sky serene,
And earth was decked in summer's sheen;
We culled bright flowers along the dells,
And from the lake fantastic shells;
Admired the lark's celestial strain,
The humbler linnet's sweet refrain,
The black-bird whistling on the oak,
And softer song the thrush awoke,
'Till soul and sense immersed in bliss,
I stoop to win one prattler's kiss:
A loud report like musket's knell,
Dissolved the fond enchanting spell;
The charmer fled, the charmed to pain,
And life's stern battle woke again;
Woke just to hear the distant hill,
Repeat the sound, then all was still.
I raised my head with watchful care,
To feast my eyes on prospect fair;
The sun was high, 'twas nearly noon,
The breeze was mild, as breeze of June,
And blew towards me from the bay,
Where two tall ships at anchor lay,
Their yards inclined in graceful ease,
And floating in the fondling breeze,
Pennant and flag, and bannerole,
In countless numbers crowned the whole.
Beyond the ships, on beach of sand,
A single tower o'erlooked the strand;

Whilst just across the narrow sound,
From bolder height the fortress frowned;
A haughty, stern, defiant mass,
The giant guardian of the pass;
Far stretching inland from the coast,
Tent after tent, and host on host,
In war's gay pagentry arrayed!
A glorious scene the eye surveyed.
A hamlet crowns the martial scene,
A thicket shades the dark ravine,
And rising from the basin's sands,
A noble pile, like temple stands,
Where floats—'Tis England's banner still,
Those are her hosts, and this the mill!
And scarce a gun-shot from my lair,
I threw me back, in mute despair;
Till softer sorrows kindly crept,
Around my heart, and long I wept.
This was no verdant, grateful bower,
Of foliage bright, of fragrant flower,
Where birds of plumage gay, and voice
Melodious, make the soul rejoice.
One flower alone usurped the dell,
Of mammoth bloom and rankest smell,
And from its glaring petals oozed,
A deadly juice, if pierced or bruised;
Each tree, that showed its blighted head,
Above the level pall, seemed dead,
And from its scathed and blasted crown,
Black, ragged wreaths of moss hung down,
Uncomely as the ghastly tress,

That decks the gibbet's rottenness.
Below, so deep the noon-day shade,
The vampire fluttered in the glade;
The vulture raised her hungry brood,
Secure amid the solitude;
The buzzard lean, that all day long,
Patrolled the camps, an army strong,
With garbage gorged, and carrion foul,
Here roosted with the hooting owl:
As night approached, whilst beasts of prey,
Roamed free and fearless night and day;
Here serpents hissed their poisoned breath,
And bloated lizards big with death,
With venom burnished, swarmed around,
Or basked in light, if light were found;
With horrid jaws and hideous tail,
And clothed in adamantine mail,
Huge alligators plunged and played,
In pitchy pools, beneath the shade.
Three traitors from the rebel-side,
To join our ranks the passage tried;
Two only reached the British host,
One in a swallow-hole got lost;
At noon of day his comrades told,
Such horrors of the dreary hold,
All shunned its precincts, named the fen,
In language strong, the Devil's Den;
And I, outlawed and desolate,
Am guardsman o'er its gloomy gate.
With thirst oppressed, tho' I have drain'd
My last sweet drop—with hunger pained;

Foes all around ; if man I flee,
Ferocious beasts await for me ;
If these I shun, upon my path,
Foul reptiles spew their venomed wrath,
Whose touch is death. If I should gain,
Unharmed from these, the open plain,
Our watchful pickets lie in wait,
To meet me at the farther gate ;
Yet not a hope remains to me,
In this, my dire extremity !
But face the perils I unfold,
And risk the passage of the hold ;
My purpose fixed upon my face,
I turned to leave my hiding place ;
When human voices reached my ear,
And chained my soul in silent fear,
Whilst from the covert where I lay,
I watched their shallop skim the bay ;
The rower ere he reached the shore,
A moment rested on his oar ;
So keenly he the land surveyed,
I deemed my hiding place betrayed.
This is, he cried, the only place,
The foot of man may hope to trace.
His comrade answered, 'tis a shore,
I little hanker to explore ;
But since no cho ce our journey waits,
Urge on beneath its dismal gates.
But what is this ? a boat is near,
Delay, till we the tidings hear ;
'Tis stern Sir Arthur waits below,

And Shane O'Neill—a friend and foe.
Ho, boatman ! cried the anxious chief,
Why urge thy voyage here ? be brief.
The rower turned around his head,
And cried, your enemy is dead !
Is that his carcass on the raft ?
The drunken boatman loudly laughed,
The alligators down the bay,
His carcass eat at break of day ;
That's Billy Milbank lying there,
He drank full twice his lawful share,
And now he claims reward entire,
His gun went off, but mine missed fire ;
O'Donnel's death upset the boat,
We found his cap and this afloat ;
We never saw him rise again ;
The alligators, that is plain,
Devoured him ; clothes and boots and all.
You lie ! his comrade now did bawl,
I saw him in the morning fog,
Your musket missed, I shot the dog ;
The money's mine ; I drank too deep,
And on the Island fell asleep,
Sir Arthur cried ; go back in haste,
And guard and iron well this beast ;
On duty drunk, reward or not,
At my return I'll have him shot !
This order carry out forthwith,
And at your deadly peril, Smith.
In sulky silence Smith made sail ;
What savage brutes are these, O'Neill ;

Yet brutes have feeling to their kind,
These, dead in soul and dark in mind,
Below the level of the beast,
Their highest aim a drunken feast;
For ever foremost of the van,
They hound a doomed, defenceless man;
Rank, craven cowards, in disguise,
They flee the first, if peril rise:
They riot, grovel, gormandize,
To honor dead—Yea, dead to grace,
The moral reptiles of the race.
Pity it were, O'Neill replied,
That by such death O'Donnel died,
And at such hands. I never knew,
A trustier hand and heart more true;
But rash in act when roused to ire,
Such was the son and such the sire.
Of great Hugh Roe, fair Ulster's pride,
No truer scion lived or died.
Unworthy boast! Sir Arthur cried;
Inglorious praise and out of place,
Yet native to thy flighty race;
What 'vails such mockery to crown,
The peasant's rags with high renown;
Dost sweeter make the beggar's bite,
To boast his father died a knight,
Or soothe the pauper's needy care,
Who dreams him still a monarch's heir,
Or chieftain of an ancient clan,
Whose sword was law—Give me the man,

Who peer or peasant fills with grace,
In rise, or fall, his present place,
Leveling his mind to changing chance,
Moulding, not mourning, circumstance.
I knew him gen'rous to a fault,
To honor true, yet blind and halt,
Where duties clothed in humbler guise,
Around life's prosier path arise;
A life to save would risk his own,
That hallowed impulse overthrown,
Just the next hour in deadly strife,
Imperilling that rescued life.
Graceful in speech, and often grave,
The fool of fools and tool of knave,
Who pandering to his fancies vain,
The secrets of his soul attain,
And prating like a silly boy,
Of great Clontarf and Fontenoy;
Of mighty Chief and Druid old,
Robbers and cheats, if truth were told;
Would level princes, peers and all,
Yet from the leveled mass would crawl,
Claiming from prostrate friend and foe,
All hail! great offshoot of Hugh Roe.
'Twere well if Patrick's high command,
And hallowed power had purged the lanc
He lived to love and blessing died,
Of barbarous chief and clannish pride.
But haste, each moment of delay,
May peril much at break of day.

Those gallant ships a goodly store,
Of guns and caissons sent on shore;
Beyond the fort our war-ships ride
At anchor, waiting for the tide;
Five thousand fighting men, all told,
In best array, the transports hold;
These added to our gallant host,
We force the fight at any cost!
O'Donnel's chase was bruited round,
To blind the spies, for spies abound,
To hide a higher aim—a ruse,
That for my absence makes excuse.
I fain would view that plain, O'Neill,
'Twixt either host, that soon shall reel
With conflict on its troubled breast,
And harbour many a stranger guest.
Sir Arthur buckled tight his brand,
And bore a musket in his hand;
Forsook the boat, and led the way;
O'Neill, a moment made delay,
Then cried aloud, 'twere better here,
Replace a portion of our cheer,
And leave behind this cum'brous spear;
His master signaled his consent,
Then both on their adventure went.
Still as a corpse, awhile I lay,
And heard their voices die away,
In distance lost—then left my lair,
To eat and drink my present care.
My feet had scarcely touched the ground,
When startled by a moaning sound,

I turned around, the cause to trace,
When lo! before me, face to face,
A monster famished wild cat stood,
And ravening on my treasured food,
Now foul'd and scattered o'er the boat;
He fiercely growling in his throat;
I must have portion of that cheer,
I dare not shout, my foes are near;
Between us lay the trusty lance:
In motion slow, I made advance;
Those fearful orbs, in angry blaze,
My steps arrest, and fix my gaze,
And as I watched those glowing eyes,
Whose rays malignant, varying dyes
Assumed; now dark, now brightest red;
All other objects hid or fled;
A savage joy, a wild desire,
Rose in my breast, my blood on fire,
Flowed like hot lava thro' my veins,
A savage courage, rules and reigns,
Yea! riots in my heart and soul,
A moment more, beyond control
The cow'ring cat with fearful yell,
And sudden spring regained the dell,
Then I, from force malignant, freed,
With famished beast's, ungracious greed,
Supplied at once, my utmost need;
I picked the fragments up in haste,
And slung the satchel 'round my waist,
Appeased my thirst from goodly store,
And filled my can to flowing o'er;

I found the spear too long, by half,
And gained a way to break the staff;
For self-defence, in tangled glade,
A handier brand was never made;
I shoved the boat, with silent oar,
A little space beyond the shore;
My purpose, should my efforts fail,
To track Sir Arthur and O'Neill,
Or, thro' the pickets reach the foe,
With knowledge, worth a mint to know;
Retrace my steps, and in the night,
Trust to the boat, for further flight;
And now I seek some keep or bay,
To hide my treasured craft away.
I think along the dreary shore,
I must have crept a mile or more,
When such a shelter, black with shade,
Yet, bordering on an open glade,
My hiding place and harbor made;
'Neath blackest shade, the boat I tied
And left. My every want supplied,
Water and food at my command,
A trusty weapon in my hand,
I sought a passage thro' the reeds,
Thro' trailing vines, and tangled weeds,
Oft forced upon my knees to crawl,
Till clamb'ring up an earthen wall,
In height and breadth resembling those,
The northern beaver's haunts disclose,
I found a pathway, dry and high,
And o'er my head, the gladsome sky,

My spirits buoyed, my heart elate,
In sturdy strength, I laughed at fate,
And half desired my haughty breast,
A foe, my steel and skill to test.
Oh! faithless breast, and veering still,
Like weather cock, 'twixt good and ill,
Pleading in peril or distress,
For heaven to aid thy helplessness;
The danger past, the want supplied,
The helper spurned, and need denied;
Thus conscience chid my guilty pride;
My sorrowing soul, the sin deplored,
And grace her rule benign, restored;
I glanced along the tangled ground,
And at a distance scanned a mound;
It seemed to be a hidden stone,
With moss of ages over grown,
To purge of pride, my guilty breast,
I knelt—my knee that hillock prest;
At once an odor foul as death,
And sickn'ing, almost choked my breath,
My gaze on sight so loathsome fell,
I shudder still, the tale to tell;
My knee was on a serpent's head,
His hellish jaws wide flaring spread,
His barbed tongue's incessant play,
Hissed at each dart, a deadly spray;
His dev'lish eyes were fixed on mine,
And round one leg his coils entwine;
Each moment adds to my distress,
So fierce the shrinking folds oppress,

But what is worse, beneath my knee,
His head recedes, 'twill soon be free;
Uncumbered by my shielding weight,
His deadly fangs will seal my fate;
My soul, the desp'rate hazard weighed,
And one tremendous effort made;
And as my knee depressed the soil,
The monster slacked his rigid coil,
From my pained limb his folds withdrew,
And quivering, stretched his length to view;
Tho' cringed his skull beneath my press,
And his foul length lay motionless,
To make assurance doubly sure,
I reached, my weapon to secure;
I touched the shaft with awkward hand,
And in the ditch upset the brand;
I gazed below with eager eyes,
From where it sank saw bubbles rise:
The pool was black, as black as night,
And heft and blade were lost to sight;
Whilst still upon my hands and knees,
I heard a rustling through the trees;
Ere on the object I could glance—
Down flat, Sir Arthur! down at once!
Shrieked out O'Neill! a moment more
Came musket shot, and savage roar;
With all the haste I dared to make,
I crept towards the tangled brake;
So dense and close, the jungle grew,
No entrance opened to my view;
A willow, bending to the ground,

Was now the only refuge found ;
Dragging along upon my breast,
Beneath its drooping boughs I pressed ;
So close o'er head the creepers clung,
So low the pendant branches hung,
When first I entered, not a ray
Illum'ed the recess where I lay,
A little while sufficed to trace,
Though indistinct, my hiding place :
Bones and decaying flesh, unclean,
Where I could see, alone were seen.
The knowledge filled my soul with care,
A savage beast's abandoned lair,
Perhaps the monster's lurking nigh ;
My foremost impulse was to fly;
But fear, more fell, of christian men,
Detained me in the horrid den ;
In half the time it takes to tell,
Yea less, what I relate, befell,
And all the time, my foes so near,
Each word they uttered, I could hear ;
O'Neill's loud call, and musket shot,
Sir Arthur answered on the spot,
With shout of startled terror, dead !
His paws in contact with my head.
Thank God in Heaven, your aim was true,
O'Neill replied : thank heaven and you,
Your action prompt, a moment staid,
Your life the forfeit would have paid.
Whilst climbing yonder wall of clay,
A portion 'neath my steps gave way,

I dropped my musket in the mire,
And fearing lest it fail in fire,
Renewed the powder in the prime;
When I the dyke again would climb,
That savage beast usurped the path,
And muttering deep his moan of wrath,
Like cat preparing for a bound,
Slow sank his body to the ground:
I took my aim, but, struck with awe,
When right in range your head I saw;
My call, a single instant lost,
We now can count the fearful cost;
He sprang as dropped your head below,
And as he sprang, received the blow;
That instant gave his dying roar.
Foul beast, your treachery is o'er!
Though many a painter felt my ball,
This is the hugest one of all.
Sir Arthur answered, load at once,
A beast more huge is in advance,
I only had a partial view,
Yon intervening thicket through,
What seemed his head, I made my aim,
Your summons urged a stronger claim;
In falling flat upon my face,
I lost, or else he fled the place;
His footprints we are sure to find:
If ready, keep a space behind.
My soul abandoned all defense,
But power of hearing grew intense,
Their foot-falls on the yielding sod,

Seemed loud and clear, as if they trod
On frozen ground—a bramble broke,
Alarmed my ear like thunder-stroke;
Their whispering council, slow and hush,
Came like a torrent's headlong gush.
Crept o'er my heart, a chill of fear,
When spoke Sir Arthur, he is here!
The sod is soft, behold, O'Neill,
Along the pool the monster's trail,
See 'neath his weight the ground gave way;
Yon drooping willow hides the prey.
This random shot may rouse his ire,
Else he attack; reserve your fire
Till I reload—twere best, you know,
Keep vantage over every foe.
Flat lying on my face and hands,
I heard the hunter's deadly plans.
Resigned to heaven my hopeless lot,
Awaited death, nor life besought;
A sudden shock my body turned
Full on my side, my temples burned,
The hot blood streaming down my face,
And near my head, an open space,
Where the fierce missile cut its way,
And ope'd to me unwelcome day;
Whilst through the open space I viewed,
With silent awe, each hunter's mood;
His musket raised, O'Neill stood by,
With lips compressed, and fiery eye;
Sir Arthur, peering through the smoke,
Down on his knees, but neither spoke.

His right hand, on the pathway pressed
Sustained his now recumbent breast,
His left, with musket raised on high,
Like balance swayed against the sky;
The hand the Baron's body stayed,
Was right upon the serpent laid;
Though crushed his head, to my surprise,
Coil after coil began to rise;
From wrist to elbow, round and round,
His sick'ning length, the reptile wound;
His folds, all powerless now to harm,
Weighed heavy on Sir Arthur's arm;
He glanced aside, his horrid yell,
Like thunder, shook the gloomy dell;
With fearful oath and frantic bound,
He flung the serpent to the ground,
Then reeling like a drunken man,
Back from the loathsome reptile ran:
O'Neill beheld his master reel,
And instant with his iron heel,
Upon the writhing monster trod,
Stamping his carcass 'neath the sod,
Then sought his master's palsied hand,
And bound the wrist with rigid band,
Cried, to the pool without delay!
We'll wash the soil and slime away;
I'll probe the wound, and suck at once,
The virus; 'tis your only chance;
My hand was wounded thus before,
O'Donnel probed it to the core;
As childhood's lips with hunger prest,

Suck nurture from the mother's breast,
His manly lips assailed with greed
The wound, until it ceased to bleed,
And poured at once the healing balm,
O'er rankling heart and poisoned palm;
They sought the pool a step below,
And bade the cleansing waters flow,
'Til not a spot, or speck, or stain
Did on that graceful hand remain ;
Then both examined round and round,
But wound or scratch was no where found ;
I would have sworn, Sir Arthur spoke,
I felt his fangs envenomed stroke,
For rushing wild thro' heart and brain,
Shot like a dart, a scorching pain,
As I relaxed my fatal grasp,
In horror from the deadly asp ;
Let's leave at once this cursed dell,
That seems the portico of hell,
Where noxious rankness rules the scene,
And every living thing unclean.
I'll face, if need, an hundred men—
My foes—ere I retrace this den.
The gun Sir Arthur cast aside ;
O'Neill, once more, with charge supplied,
And gave his own, of shorter range,
But weighing less, back in exchange ;
An instant more, and both were gone
From sight, and sound—and I alone ;
Crushed in that den's unhallowed space,
My life-blood streaming down my face,

My hands besmeared with blood and mire,
My garments foul'd, my brow on fire!
I crept, and in the pitchy pool,
My head immersed, my brow to cool;
In lonely, hopeless agony,
Then laid me on the brink, to die;
But forced, so fiercely throbbed my brain,
To bathe my brow, again, again.
As if within the wave there lay,
A charm, to banish pain away,
And staunch the blood; it ceased to flow,
Waxed less and less, the burning glow,
And hope, within my heart her reign
Restored, as fled the fiery pain.
A mirror of the pool I made,
And in its depth my face surveyed;
A line upon my forehead seared,
As if by burning brand, appeared,
And in the centre oozing blood,
An ugly, bloated blister stood;
A prickly bramble, seen by chance,
Supplied me with a needful lance;
On either side a puncture made,
Another flow of blood essayed;
A linen strip lay on the ground,
That late, the Baron's wrist had bound,
So near, I reached it with my hand,
And swathed my temples with the band;
I purified my hands and clothes,
And on my feet at last arose,
To try whatever fate ordain,

For life and liberty again.
I followed close, my foes advance,
With cautious step and watchful glance,
Before, behind, on either side,
And once I laid me down to hide,
So true my fancy ruled by fear,
Upon the track bade both appear;
The way, a swampy level crossed,
Here track and trail at once I lost;
I shunned each quagmire's gaping trap,
And crossed, tho' tired without mishap,
A jungle closed to light of day,
And seeming trackless barr'd my way,
As 'neath its twisted boughs I crawled,
There came a sound my heart appalled;
Some beast of prey, my fears portrayed;
I glanced behind me, to the glade
I just had left—Oh! blissful sight,
That filled my soul with sweet delight,
Renewed my hopes, allayed my fears,
A playful rabbit pricks his ears;
The noise, my hasty turning made,
His dreaded enemy betrayed,
I kissed my hand, as if to say,
Poor thing no harm from me to-day;
An instant more, he urged his flight,
And in the thicket fled my sight.
The mind alert from slender sign,
Will things of import, oft divine,
And I, in pusses presence read,
Ferocious beasts no more to dread.

In haste her foot-steps I pursue,
At every step my hopes renew,
I trace a track, with sward as green,
And lovely, as an old boreen;
Where at each turn, caught unawares,
Sometimes alone, and oft in pairs,
The timid creatures wildered stand,
Till I might touch them with my hand,
The pleasant path's bewitching calm,
Like sinful pleasure's poison-balm,
That lures to ruin, lulled to sleep,
That vigilance, I still should keep;
Like thunder-stroke, as sudden fell,
The challange of a sentinel,
Halt! and your name. A voice replied,
St. Clair. The pass—"Let traitors hide."
Who follows near! I deemed to me,
This challenge came. I just could see,
The watchful picket's leveled gun,
Bright gleaming in the setting sun;
'Tis Shane O'Neill, broke forth St. Clair,
I placed on sentry in the rear:
My purpose, through the lines to steal,
I now commend your watchful zeal.
He bade his orderly advance,
I, watchful for a friendly chance,
Within the thicket made my lair,
Not half a bow shot from St. Clair,
Who, of the sentinel would know,
The latest tidings from the foe;
Some change he makes, the guard replied,

Close were his wing last eventide,
Like bended bow in warrior's hand,
His center, on yon hill of sand ;
His right and left extending near,
Our guards their bugles' call could hear;
Their center still rests on the height,
Their wings withdrawn, are lost to sight.
Go, tell the captain of your band,
At once, that I, St. Clair, command
He forward here with instant speed,
Two horses, saddled for our need,
At our return : Now haste O'Neill,
The day, too soon, begins to fail,
From yonder hill, we yet may gain,
The knowledge I would like attain.
With throbbing heart, from where I lay,
I saw my foemen move away ;
The picket passing to the right,
Was in a moment lost to sight,
Whilst to the front, and down the vale,
Set forth Sir Arthur and O'Neill.
I to the left and through the brake,
King George's hosts and cause forsake,
And tears of joy within the dell,
My cheeks bedewed, at my farewell ;
I kept the thicket's darkest screen,
'Til died the day, and stars were seen,
But ray more dear than rising star,
From proud Columbia's hosts of war,
With transport filled my soul, as blaze
An hundred watchfires to my gaze,

I hold as nought that burning pain,
That oft comes throbbing thro' my brain,
My bounding heart's pulsations true,
I hear. My limbs their strength renew,
On! on I press, nor feel the thorn,
That from my face the flesh has torn,
Thro' rocky dells, I force a pass,
Turn not, to shun the deep morass;
The hill that hides my beacon fires,
I climb, and not a muscle tires,
Like mountain torrent swelled with rain,
In headlong haste, I seek the plain;
Stop not to choose of path or track,
But seek the nearest bivouac,
Yet staid a-back a narrow space,
And cried aloud for truce and grace.
The dells alone repeat the prayer,
No living soul responded there;
From fire to fire, along the line,
I turned my gaze to catch some sign
Of sentinel, the watch-fires' rays,
Unbroken ever, mocked my gaze.
Just then upon a summit high,
A rising beacon caught my eye,
Broad, bright and glorious spread the blaze,
Like bonfire of my boyhood's days,
And round that glorious beacon stand,
Of stalwart forms a goodly band;
I fixed the distance at a guess,
To be an English mile or less.
Like will o-wisps, are hill-top fires

At night. Approach the hill retires,
For lower heights hide in the shade,
And valleys lie in ambuscade ;
And torrents heard, but all unseen,
With dangerous ford, and deep ravine,
May lie with many a mile between,
Hills, vales and dreary dark defiles,
My journey lengthened into miles,
And when at last the hill I gained,
Ashes, and smoking brands remained.
And giant forms half hid in gloom,
Whose every helmet waves a plume,
I plaintive urge my dreary need,
For mercy, rest, and succor, plead,
I deemed each warrior turned at once,
And bent on me enquiring glance ;
Toward the group I nearer drew,
Swore solemn plight my tale was true,
And I, all weaponless you see,
I raised both hands and bent my knee
In dread suspense, and filled with fear,
My doom, for life, or death to hear.
The autumn wind in fitful gale,
Spoke loud and sad, like funeral wail,
Revived the embers into flame,
And filled my soul with woe and shame.
Dumb, hideous effigies of men,
In martial trappings, mocked my ken,
In soul-sick anguish, on my face,
I threw me down, and wept apace.
How long I lay I cannot tell,

A sleep and horrid night-mare spell,
My soul and sense a while enfold
In agony, I leave untold;
I started up! the hills around,
Were echoing back a thundering sound,
And from my lips, unbidden fell,
Fierce imprecation, death and hell!
My dream's, sore agony and fear,
A dread reality appear,
And to my anguished soul, the seal
Of doom, unending doom, reveal;
Huge beams, like straws by whirlwind driven,
In ruin blur the face of heaven;
An instant more, like fiery rain,
Fall, crashing back to earth again.
Those foul, unsightly effigies,
Some black with smoke, and some ablaze,
Each loathsome shape of hell assume,
Now fiends, now partners of my doom;
The twinkling of an eye, unrolled
This scene of horrors I have told,
For on the instant, through the smoke
And fire, like fiend unchained, I broke,
With long, loud yell of fierce despair,
My garb ablaze, on fire my hair:
The flaming robe, I from me flung,
But round my wrist a selvage clung,
The furious wind the garment spread,
Like hell's red banner o'er my head,
To quench my burning locks I strove,
But hardest of my trials prove,

From recent wound the band to tear,
That blood and fire had welded there
A diadem of burnished flame,
Might hell's apostate prince proclaim ;
Whilst my wild shrieks, and frantic pace,
Bespeak me of that hopeless race.
A stern command, like thunder broke,
From ruined timbers' smoulder ing smoke,
And fixed me speechless to the spot,
" Foul fiend, avaunt ! I fear thee not,
Behold ! my sacred panoply ;
Thee and thy legions I defy."
A cross of brilliants, bright as day,
Reflected back my banner's ray;
Such cross the Knights of Malta bore,
On crest and shield in days of yore,
Such glorious gems I often scann'd,
On hilt of proud Sir Arthur's brand :
The hem gave way, that long confined,
The garment to my wrist, the wind
At once out spread each burning fold,
It rose on high a sheet of gold,
Then on the smouldering timbers fell,
As sank the gale in softer swell.
From splintered beams, and sable smoke,
A sudden conflagration broke;
And what before the gloom concealed,
Now bright as noon day sun revealed ;
Amid that ruin'd structure there,
Reclined my deadly foe, St. Clair !
His up-raised hand, the steel enclosed,

And hilt and cross to me opposed.
'Tis he ! I muttered, and alone,
This hour of vengeance will atone,
Insult and suffering—forth at once,
I seek the else, proud man advance.
I grasped, in rage, a burning brand,
And for the conflict took my stand ;
He cried aloud, in Jesus' name,
Tell what thou art ? and whence you came ?
If fiend, flee hence, and ne'er return,
If mortal, then thy threat I spurn !
I flew towards him, filled with rage,
That murder only, could assuage ;
I swung my blazing club in air,
War to the death ! I cried, St. Clair.
He raised him not, to shield the blow,
I dare not strike a prostrate foe ;
He spoke no word—but in his hand,
Held by the naked steel, the brand,
And kissed the cross of peace and grace,
Mute gazing on my frightful face.
Arise ! proud England's belted knight,
Arise ! and God defend the right :
Oh ! wretched man, he cried—Oh ! sight
Appalling, sad—Oh ! piteous plight,
O'Donnel thou—And still in life ?
Forbear ! bold man, this sinful strife,
Swell not your sins' unshriven roll,
With murder foul to brand thy soul ;
If life and safety be thy aim,
Not red revenge, behold yon flame !

Back from its potent wave retire,
And view, with awe, my funeral pyre;
Chained in this wreck, to death betrayed,
No foe I fear, no friend may aid;
Few moments fill my measured span,
May Heaven forgive a sinful man,
And shrive my soul; as I, St. Clair,
All men forgive, to make repair.
Whilst terror reigned, and rage ruled high,
I had not bent a downward eye;
But now his speech, reproving, calm,
Fell on my soul, like sacred balm;
I saw what first I failed to see,
His sore distress and jeopardy.
Upon one foot Sir Arthur stood,
The other crushed 'twixt beams of wood,
And wedged secure; his body bent,
Against a slanting piller leant;
His helmet still upon his head,
He seemed at ease, on rugged bed,
Whilst all below with blood was red;
The flaming tempest worked its way,
Close to the timbers where he lay,
The heat intense, altho' the wind
Opposed its course, and part confined;
Impaled upon the burning boom,
Resigned he lay awaiting doom,
Spoke no complaint, made no appeal,
My heart, tho' fire, was not of steel;
I flung the deadly club aside,
To move the beam, in vain I tried,

Not twenty men with strength, unskill'd,
That giant labor had fulfilled;
Amid the wreck I moved around,
A long, straight, tap'ring pole I found,
Full twenty feet or more in length,
Of iron heft, and stubborn strength;
Between my foeman and the flame,
I found a mortice in the beam;
Placed here my lever, as I planned;
Like boy on ladder, hand on hand,
High from the ground my body hung,
And to the end I slowly swung,
But ere I measured half the way,
Like beam, the pole began to sway;
A sudden jerk! and on the ground,
Beneath the pole, myself I found;
I sought St. Clair—the limb was free,
But crushed from ancle to the knee;
I bore him from the burning mass,
And laid him gently on the grass,
And all the while no word he spoke,
A single groan the silence broke;
His helpless arms, by either side,
Fell motionless—his pulse I tried;
Life's subtle index, throbbed not there,
And thou art dead! I cried, St. Clair;
Dead! in thy bitter foes embrace,
This doth all enmity erase;
Soft be thy slumber in the grave,
Rest to thy soul, thou warrior brave!
Unbending stern, and ever true,

To Erin's faith. St. Clair, adieu.
Tears came, I tried not to control,
And solemn musings filled my soul,
And heaven I thanked, whose mercy plann'd,
From murder foul to keep my hand.
It was not theft, it was not greed,
But want of weapon in my need,
That from his waist bade me unbind,
The leathern belt, his brand confined;
I raised his head against my knee,
The girdle's buckle to get free,
And pulled the belt, he raised his hand,
And from the scabbard drew the brand,
Thank thee O'Neil, he slowly spoke,
As if from dream he just awoke,
This ancient usage I would share,
In common with each sleeping heir,
Of our brave founder Hugh St. Clair;
Thus when my spirit shall have fled,
Replace the hemlet on my head,
My face towards the East oppose,
Thence Bethlehem's star of hope arose;
Direct my hand, the right, tho' cold,
As if in life my brand to hold;
Some bud or leaf of fragrance rare,
In honor of our Lady fair,
Should grace my left; and let it rest,
In this array, across my breast—
Oh! helpless clay, oh! faithless mind,
That racks my soul, and this how blind;
Thanks, Hugh O'Donnel for thy deed,

Of more than mercy in my need,
Helpless and doomed, you stay'd your hand,
Uplifted—at your foes command;
And all unsought, with noble grace,
Redeemed me from that fearful place ;
Oh ! how shall I that debt atone.
Thanks I disclaim, and debt disown,
I sullen spoke ; had thou been free ;
A ruthless foe were found in me,
A heart of stone, at your distress,
Would melt who saw your wretchedness;
And mine is human, tho' in ire,
Its coolest drop is liquid fire ;
No worthy son of great Hugh Roe,
E'er trampled on a prostrate foe,
Or meanly turned an idle ear,
To human suff'ring, need or fear ;
Of broad domain and titles reft,
This honored birthright still is left ;
Dear as the apple of our eye,
We guard to give, what none may buy,
But friend and foe, alike may claim,
In our great chieftain's honored name.
He raised his helmet o'er his head,
I spurn, he cried, great chieftain dead !
Dead do I say—on deathless page
Emblazoned, warrior, patriot, sage ;
I spurn my own imperfect chart,
Of that deep sea, the human heart;
And homage true, I thee bestow,
Thou sire of heroes, great Hugh Roe !

And Hugh O'Donnel, hail to thee,
Fair scion of a princely tree,
True type of true nobility.
Go seek—ere darker shadows veil
The scene; thy kinsman, Shane O'Neill!
We sought by sep'rate paths, this height,
I took the left, and he, the right.
The wounded Knight turned on his side,
And raised his hand, my steps to guide;
I followed, where he gave me sign,
And clambered up a steep incline,
Each object clearly met my eye,
As if the sun shone in the sky;
Tho' oft there fell a ghastly shade,
That o'er the scene like specter played,
When from the burning ruin broke,
Triumphant waves of sable smoke.
Where lay St. Clair, a boy might stand,
And fling a pebble with his hand,
To where sad scene, my wand'rings staid,
My mission closed, my search repaid;
Lay on the track as marble pale,
The mortal part of Shane O'Neill,
The soul to Him, who gave it, fled,
Its house of clay untenanted,
Yet, in such order and repair,
As showed propitious farewell there.
Flung by the mine's, exploding wrath,
A beam of timber plowed the path,
A splint, in passing caught his side,
And tore an opening deep and wide,

O'Neill, well used to scenes of blood,
Knew life was ebbing with the flood;
Drew from the wound the splint of pine,
And made a cross of rude design;
A lock of hair, the splinters tied,
And deep with gore, the wood was dyed.
There on his bare and manly breast,
That holy symbol lay at rest;
A smile like childhood's soft repose,
Serene, o'er all his features glows;
The fatal beam sustained his head,
Along its length, his arms were spread,
There on his fresh made couch of clay,
In voiceless speech he seemed to say,
Here, Christ my King, in holy love,
His servant called, his faith to prove;
Here on my cross, at his request,
Pleased with the call, I sink to rest.
My soul oppressed with woe, my brain,
From wound and burns, distraught with pain,
I did not touch his lonely bier,
Nor shed one tributary tear;
Forgot a christian's prayer to say,
But to his master made my way,
To him, the tidings would unfold,
But pent up woe, in wave up rolled,
And drowned in tears, my troubled tale,
I only uttered, poor O'Neill.
Dead! cried St. Clair, the fatal stroke,
That scathed the willow, fell'd the oak,
Brave man, farewell; accept the tear,

That friendship gives to gild thy bier;
Thou model monitor, and guide,
To see thy lifeless form denied,
Thy death, untimely, I deplore,
The wounded Knight, at once I bore,
And laid him by his own command,
Where he conld grasp the palsied hand.
He gazed in sorrow on the dead;
In silent prayer, he bowed his head,
Then raised to heaven, his hands on high,
And fixed his vision on the sky;
My sinful soul, I bow with awe,
This scene surpasses nature's law.
Death, thine, no dreary conquest here,
The hero triumphs on his bier,
This cross, his shield; his armour faith,
The Christian warrior conquerd death.
St. Clair, beside the corse reclined,
And to himself his thoughts confined,
I, on the other hand in woe,
Kept silent vigil with my foe.
My temples buried in my hands,
I strove to re-arrange my plans,
But all unfit to bear the strain,
The mind would loose its grasp again;
And like a lost and wand'ring wight,
In trackless waste at dead of night,
Who taxed his failing strength to find,
The haven pictured to his mind,
Finds each adventure brings him back,
More wildered on his former track;

So did my every effort end,
In sorrowing o'er my earliest friend;
And oft my troubled soul confessed,
Its agony, and sad unrest.
The burning pile, now waned in power
And darker shadows ruled the hour,
My grief, tho' poignant, felt decay,
For sleep my senses stole away,
When spoke St. Clair, behold the day!
The tidings broke my troubled dream;
I started from the shivered beam,
And saw the dim and misty rays,
The first—returning day displays;
My kinsman's nerveless hand I pressed,
A brief and sad adieu confessed,
Prayed heaven proud England's path of blood,
Might fail in ruin's darker flood,
Defeat, disaster, flight and shame,
O'erwhelm her hosts, and cloud her fame.
I pressed my lips on that cold brow,
And bade the dead, record my vow,
What cause so'eer, what daring band,
'Gainst perjured England raised the hand,
That cause was mine, my brothers, those,
Her foes my friends, her allies foes.
My blood was up, and thou St. Clair,
Her minister of ill, beware!
If you survive, live but to feel,
If e'er we meet, my heart is steel,
This be my witness, that be thine,
I tore apart the holy sign,

That lay across my kinsman's heart ;
I saw St. Clair in horror start,
I flung the wood against his face—
At such a time, and in such place,
Oh, deed unblest, the Baron cried,
Oh, suffering Lord, who for us dyed
The crosses wood, on Calvary's hill,
Look mildly down in mercy still,
And for this sacrilegious deed,
Let thine own words of mercy plead ;
Forgive this man, with many woes
Distraught ; he knows not what he does,
Reason, by rage dethroned—restore,
On heart and soul in mercy pour,
Contritious wave of balm once more ;
Thy cross, I kiss, and thee adore.
He pressed the croslet's slender tree,
With revered kiss, and gazed on me.
That act of love and prayer, he said,
Poured coals of shame upon my head,
My guilty conscience bade me yield,
But pride, my bane, my bosom steeled,
And still was master of the field.
The brighter dawn with crimson ray,
Now heralded the God of day,
Whilst conscious guilt compelled me
The pleading look he bent on me. flee,
I, glad of pretext, grasped a stave,
And turned around to scoop a grave ;
The fatal beam that wrought his doom,
Had partly built its victim's tomb ;

The trench it plowed—I made his bed,
I smoothed the pillow for his head;
As best I could I laid him there,
Then stole a glance towards St. Clair;
He caught my eye, and instant said,
Be benediction with the dead ;
And to the living, lengthened lease
Of life and health, thro' years of peace.
This deed of christian sepulture,
By christian hands, will Heaven allure ;
And sins, tho' fearful in array,
And number countless, blot away.
He held to me the crimson gage,
Of vengeful strife, flung in my rage.
Unite again, this sacred sign
Of peace, of grace, symbol divine;
Seal of thy sleeping kinsman's faith,
In life his hope, his shield in death.
To rob the dead were grievous ill,
And of the cross, more grievous still;
But sacrilege, that cross to rend,
The cross of Christ and to what end?
Remorse had swelled my heart before,
But now, the fountain bubbled o'er.
Obedient to his grave command,
I took the splinter from his hand ;
I placed the beam against the post,
The band that tied the parts was lost;
I sought the fillet to regain,
Searched all around, searched all in vain.
St. Clair, my search and purpose guessed,

And taking from beneath his vest,
A slender cord and silver cross,
Let this, he said, replace the loss;
This cross, my lovely Ellen's care,
Bestowed at parting; this, her hair,
Pressed to his lips the cross and braid,
Two truant tears his soul betrayed;
Tho' casque of iron cased his heart,
Betrayed the secret—softer part.
Twin, symbols of a Saviour's grace,
I, on my kinsman's bosom place.
With sorrowing heart and falt'ring hand,
His grave began to fill with sand;
At the first scoop I flung below,
St. Clair, in cadence sad and slow,
The sacred Deprofundis sung,
Intoning in the Latin tongue,
Then vocal made the morning breeze,
Chanting the holy litanies;
Whilst I, in under tone repeat,
The pleading soul's responses meet.
The chant was o'er, my labor done,
When, clothed in crimson, rose the sun,
And bathed the hill-top where we lay,
With promise of a glorious day.
My purpose fixed, my plans were laid,
To England's foe to flee for aid;
But morning's misty mantle still
Enrobed low vale, and lesser hill;
And restless there, and racked with pain
I tarried yet, my course to gain.

As oft is told in fairy tale,
How, when the Geni lifts the veil
From magic mirror, mortals gaze,
On scenes and sights, the soul amaze;
So when the vapory veil withdrew,
And hill and plain exposed to view,
I saw a sight, imposing, grand,
Fair as the scenes of fairy land;
To me appalling—far and near,
Blazed banner, bayonet and spear,
Horse men and foot, in proud array,
The British host before me lay;
Look to the West—I raised my hand,
Behold, St. Clair! thy whole command;
Too late! he cried, the die is cast,
Lost is our latest chance, and last:
The gem is reft from England's crown,
In dark defeat, her sun goes down;
Down, let her cause and cohorts go,
I cried; in ruin, shame and woe,
Down! Albion's pride, and freedom's foe,
Down, deep and sudden, drunk with blood,
Of martyred saints, to long she's stood,
In power, as infamy, sublime;
Mammon, her God, her incense crime,
Her altars, reared on kingdoms' graves,
Her victims, and her votaries slaves,
Crushed human hearts her sacrifice,
And she herself, high priest of lies;
I shook my fist against the sky,
And ye, her minions I defy,

My hour of vengence I pursue
Unfaltering still. St. Clair, adieu.
Stay! cried the Baron, madman, stay!
Nor vainly throw thy life away,
Where dost thou purpose hence to go?
Where, but to England's conquering foe;
Where freemen battle for the right,
'Gainst hireling slaves, I go to fight.
Oh! wretched man returned St. Clair,
Thy more than reckless risk forbear,
Those you would seek you cannot find;
Or, if some followers lurk behind,
These are in every camp the worst,
Marauders fierce, and thieves accurst,
All cowardly, cruel. What thou'st said
I bury with thy kinsman dead.
Partners in pain, our feud erase,
And of thy generous aid—and grace,
Bestowed thy Chief in direst need;
In council, I thy cause shall plead,
And on the honor of a Knight,
Restore thy soldier's rank and right,
Yea more, to thy Brigade proclaim,
The wrong was mine, and mine the shame,
—See muffled in that cloud of sand,
A force of rebel horse at hand,
Take these, and seek the British host,
He sought his tablets, they were lost;
Lost all his records; from its place,
He drew his watch, and ope'd the case,
And on the inner plate of gold,

With pen of steel his message told.
This to my first Lieutenent show ;
I, to thy-self, the toy bestow,
To me the jeweled gift he tost,
Leave me at once, or both are lost,
I wavered still—that instant broke
A volley fierce, thro' flame and smoke,
Our foremost musketeers had laid,
For these rough riders, ambuscade ;
But sand and dust, in airy speed,
Had far outstripped the fastest steed,
And all too soon the volley sped.
The foremost rider's horse fell dead,
Beside St. Clair; then slaughter red,
With vengeful hand her banner spread.
Like bolt of death shot from the bow,
The horsemen hurl them on the foe,
Down the defile, and rugged road,
Ere one in ten their guns reload,
Like tempest thunder on their flank,
Like whirlwind sweep their closer rank ;
Cut thro' the stunn'd, disordered mass,
Beyond the gorge's narrow pass,
Then wheeling on the open plain,
Charge with a cheer, the dell again.
The braver few in order close,
And gallantly their course oppose,
By blow, by bayonet and ball;
Three riders with their horses fall ;
But the fierce press that swells below,
Tramps fallen friend and reckless foe.

Broad sword and saber hew their way,
Steeds crush the dying where they lay,
The braver few that boldly stay,
The baser throng that runs away ;
All, all with usury repay,
The levy of the opening fray.
Four horsemen fell, whilst of our band,
Four score and ten who ambush plann'd,
And ill-advised, invoked the strife,
Three only barely 'scaped with life,
And all were maimed ; filled with amaze,
I on the conflict fixed my gaze,
Forgetting that I trod the edge
Of torrent's brink, on crumbling ledge ;
I missed a step, and backward sank,
Then all, for many weeks is blank.
The soldier paused a little here,
Stopped by the chasm in his career :
Wiped with his sleeve the drops of spray,
That on his swarthy forehead lay ;
Rose from his seat, removed his coat,
And took the collar off his throat ;
As if the coat were cloth of gold,
Or robe of state, he pressed each fold,
Each wrinkle smoothed, in order fair,
Then graced once more his vacant chair.
I said that weeks had come and passed,
And I unconscious ; when at last
The dormant mind, its powers renewed,
There, Hugh O'Donnel, near me stood,
And gazed in silence on my face.

With anxious look—I scanned the place.
There shone the window, barred and high,
But open else, to air and sky;
The open door, a space ajar,
I know those iron studs, and bar;
I turned my gaze along the floor,
And traced the outlines of the door;
This is the self-same prison cell,
And here my former sentinel;
And I, as on that fatal day,
Save that upon a cot I lay
Unmanacled—in durance still;
Through all my being, shot a thrill
Of deepest anguish, dread and shame,
The doom is real, the rest a dream;
I screamed in terror—Where am I?
The sentinel made no reply;
I raised me up—Where is St. Clair?
And Shane O'Neill? Oh! tell me where?
He bent and whispered in my ear,
Namesake and comrade, nothing fear,
The worst is past; from jeopardie,
Of doom and fever, thou art free;
I am thy nurse, this thy old cell,
St. Clair is prisoner; what befell
Thy kinsman brave, I cannot tell,
His former comrades, all but me,
In thy sad guise thy kinsman see;
And pity shattered Shane O'Neill,
'Twere dangerous yet to lift the veil,
He laid me down and bade me keep,

The secret safe and try to sleep,
Then hailed a comrade as he passed,
O'Neill, Is now himself at last.
Indignant at the guile, I cried,
My honored name I ne'er denied;
He closed the door against the guard,
And in the cell the portal barred ;
Grasped where I lay my wasted hand,
And further speech and protest bannd ;
Told how he found me where I lay,
The evening of that fatal day,
That saw St. Clair, a prisoner made,
My head and hands and features flayed,
My body bruised, bereft of mind,
Breathing, but helpless mute and blind.
How all my comrades scann'd me well,
But none my name or rank could tell,
Till they had raised me from the ground ;
When, where I fell a watch was found,
Sir Arthur's arms and ancient crest,
Embossed with gold their gaze arrest,
Then all amazed, with pity hail,
In me, the wreck of Shane ONeill.
Spoke of that band with rapine red,
Still mourning o'er their comrade dead ;
Deeming me shot, consign their foe,
To regions of unending woe,
And seeking still the helping hand,
That foiled their deed of murder plann'd,
If found unpitying fate prevails,
Their motto, " dead men tell no tales ;"

Till we can counsel with St Clair,
Let no one else the secret share,
Comrade! he cried, 'tis almost night,
Dost thou assent, I gave my plight.
He shook my hand with friendly press,
Then raised me up, my wounds to dress,
My lips with fitting nurture fed;
Then smoothed my pillow and my bed.
The bugles mellow notes arose,
Proclaiming evening's blest repose,
To Christian hearts in every clime,
That bugle call, or holier chime,
Of bells, in high cathedral tower,
Proclaims our Lady's vesper hour;
In peace—the prince and peasant kneel,
Obedient to the hallowed peal,
Mother and child, like bud and blow,
That with heaven's fragrant dews o'er flow,
And droop in sweetness; at the sound,
In lowly meekness kiss the ground,
In homage to a brighter flower,
The Regal Rose of Sharon's bower.
The sailor on the deep, deep, sea,
That emblem of eternity;
From his heart's ocean culls a gem,
To grace his Lady's diadem.
The soldier mid the battle's blaze,
His heart and helmet both will raise,
Blots from his mind death's harvest field,
By wars rude husbandry assailed;
Its golden grain with blood defiled,

And sheaf and shock in ruin piled;
His soul upraised, will mutely trace,
Great Gabriel's words of wonderous grace,
And bend like him, the willing knee,
To Mary; maid of Galilee.
And I, a wav'ring wandering child,
My soul with guilt of years defiled;
What could a son so faithless, bring
Bankrupt in worthy offering,
To purity's eternal spring:
Flower of all flowers of fragrance Queen,
Bright ocean star of ray serene,
Fountain of pity, that o'er flows,
With wave of balm for human woes;
A wounded heart I brought to thee,
Fond filial love, true fealty
Renewed—in suffering sanctified,
Repentant tears, and wounded pride;
But enemies stole unawares,
And o'er the fallow scattered tares,
The good, a stunted crop is found,
The tares in rankest growth abound.
I closed my eyes, and tried to raise,
My grateful soul in silent praise;
To God's Omniscient care resigned,
The hopes and fears that moved my mind;
Resolved no more in vain complaint,
His will oppose, lest I should faint,
Or fail in strength, I humbly prayed,
Our blessed Mother's loving aid.
Then tyrant nature rose in might,

Forced reason from her throne of light,
Took of her fair domain control,
And chained in sleep my captive soul.
Yet, left as suits a royal ward,
Of gentle friends, an honored guard ;
But every portal tripple barr'd.
The soldier paused and ranged his eye,
Around the board as if to pry.
Within each silent listener's breast,
If faith or doubt, their looks confessed,
From every eye assuring rays,
Of trust confiding, blessed his gaze ;
The iron sternness of his face,
Seemed softening into lines of grace,
And happier thoughts his mind beguile,
His lips are melting with a smile
He tries to strangle, but in vain,
And thus pursues his tale again :
My gentle friends will pardon me,
This unbecoming levity ;
For as they met my mortal eyes,
On memory's mirror scenes arise,
The sweet and sad, the grave and gay,
And on the heart's Æolien play,
Woe sweeps the strings, whilst folly waits,
The opening of the wizard gates,
To trill the chords that grief vibrates.
Such scenes I fain would pass aside,
To bridge my story's gap, I tried ;
But still I see that ragged band,
And hear their leader's mock command.

Comrade! broke forth the stranger youth,
Thy tale is strange, none doubts its truth;
Its sterner trials woke our fears,
Its darker sorrows, claimed our tears;
Those lighter scenes, of liv'lier cheer,
Comrade, awake! we wait to hear.
He gleans from all approving smiles,
And thus the wintry day beguiles:
The sun toward the west inclined,
Ere sleep, her lengthened rule resigned,
And I awoke, from suffering free,
Blessed by the sweet captivity;
Awoke to wonder, how the day,
Had, whilst I slumbered, passed away!
I deemed I heard the sentry's tread,
And to the door I turned my head,
The profile of a human face,
Pressed to the jamb, at once I trace.
The head, decked in fantastic style,
The features, warped in funny smile,
The only eye that I could see,
Bent on my face, and lit with glee,
And twinkling, like a frosty star,
He broke the silence. Powers of war!
Who e'er beheld so sweet a face,
Adorned with such becoming grace.
Comrades! he turned his head aside,
And to his boon companions cried,
Then in the chamber took his stand,
And introduced his motley band,
In single file. He named them o'er,

Each name a heathen God's of yore;
With Jupiter, the roll began,
In order of succession ran;
Of deities, a decade named,
Cupid, with wings, himself proclaimed,
Spread pinions of his tattered clothes,
From all the crew a cheer arose.
Still one, a giant, stood behind,
His name and virtues undefined,
An iron pot his head adorns,
On either side rose bullock's horns;
A mask of crape o'erspread his face,
And in his hand he held a mace,
Leaned on a staff, with triple prong,
And sung in doleful tones, a song;
His comrades swelled this chorus strain,
To every stanzas last refrain:
John Bull, my cousin, ran away,
Yankee doodle dandy;
And left the devil here to pay—
Singing, sweets of candy—
The song and singers all disclose,
Their sympathy with England's foes.
I questioned not, the truth to ken,
That these were Yankee bummer-men;
A race thrown up by war's wild tide,
Oft stranded, as the waves subside;
The scum aud dregs, and putrid rack,
That mark its devastating track;
Fierce wolves by night, foxes by day,
On friend and foe, alike they prey,

The needy rob, the weak oppress,
And glory in each vile excess.
Cupid, the leader of the band,
As sign of silence, raised his hand,
And when they hushed their loud acclaim,
Bade me unfold my rank and name.
In tones assumed, but sharp and stern,
Their cause and calling I would learn;
The spokesman gave me back reply—
Our cause is great—our calling high;
Freedom's evangelists are we,
In days of ancient chivalry,
Knights errant hight; this iron age,
Slighting our honored heritage
And high renown, basely requites
Our deeds, and names us erring knights;
We vigils keep, like monks of old,
But love to *prey* on beads of gold;
The rigid rules of *cannon* law,
Inspire our brotherhood with awe,
Our fastings mortify the man,
Against our feasting there is bann.
Where mammon gilds the house of sin,
The *golden* angels woo us in;
The callous rich we oft persuade,
Our weary pilgrimage's aid.
With subtle *points*, we move the soul,
That alms denied to give the whole,
We clothe the naked—from the hook
Where long it hung, my coat he took,
And gave it to his comrade Mar;

Said, this becomes the God of war,
We feed the hungry without fee,
Turn round your radiant face and see;
I turned around upon a board,
Beside my cot were viands stored,
Left there by friendly hand unknown,
When slumber claimed me as her own,
Like hungry wolves, as fierce and fast,
Of all my store they made repast,
Nor left for me the smallest crumb;
I turned away appall'd and dumb,
Cursed in my heart that cruel band,
When on my head was placed a hand,
Blest mortal thou who feasts the Gods,
Jove crowns thee king in land of nods,
And he, our potentate of lies,
That England's George did canonize,
Proclaims, thy flesh unknown to taint,
And thee our tutelary saint;
St. Bummer's name, the roll adorns,
Behold! the Bull—in yonder horns.
In pain I turned my head aside,
Peace, great celestial peace, he cried!
Then from my head the band untied,
And to his ruffian ragged crew,
Sir Arthur's watch exposed to view;
Its chain of gold and ruby seal,
I deemed he said an idle tale,
That proverb in my youth I read,
"The toad has jewels in his head;"
Time's golden dial proves that truth,

Which I held fable in my youth ;
He placed the watch against his ear,
A tapster's motto, no *tick*, here,
St. Clair's armorial bearings met,
His gaze, by jove a coronet,
Of great Sir John, of high renown,
No kin; I'll bet a British crown ?
Falstaff in strategy would lie,
Pierced with his wit, his foes would die :
Ill-tempered blades are seldom bright,
And dullness still belongs by right
Of nature, to an ill star'd night ;
I closed my eyes, repose in sleep,
He cried, the Gods thy watch will keep,
Thou dimi-dandy—lying God,
Great monarch in the land of nod,
We leave thee in thy royal ease,
Blest with thy body guard of fleas.
When his rude homily was o'er;
His comrades wakened such a roar,
Hip, hip Hurrah! cheer after cheer,
As pierced the soul, and pained the ear,
And made the empty walls reply,
In echo to the horrid cry.
The noisy wave had spent its force,
When other cry, less loud, less hoarse,
From distant chamber rose on high,
But this was pleading plaintive cry,
Hark ! Cupid cried, a lady calls,
Immured within these dreary halls ;
Flee Mercury on wings of fear,

And guide the lovely captive here,
We'll have the ransomed damosel,
Before the Gods her torture tell.
He turned to me, Justice is blind,
Should we a second Blue Beard find—
Ho, Ho! a man, the jester said,
As Billy Milbank showed his head;
His ancle clasped with iron band,
The clanking chain, borne in his hand,
Both fat and sleek with food and ease,
But weak and trembling at the knees.
He gazed in terror round the room,
Awaiting, silently, his doom,
Till Cupid, bowing with mock grace,
Cried, "Morning, Mr. Boniface;"
You keep a watch and chain, I see,
Good time, and honest company.
A trumpet, on the instant heard,
With hoarse command—Turn out the guard!
At once, the comedy cut short,
And terror took the place of sport;
Each ruffian-hand his mask withdrew,
And villainy stood full in view,
Theft, arson, rapine, murder fell,
And coward; writ indelible
On every face, with burning brand.
Stand! at your deadly peril, stand!
Who moves a foot, I seal his doom!
The speaker strode within the room;
A huge horse pistol graced his hand,
The right one grasped a heavy brand,

His sun-burnt face and martial air,
Proclaim the veteran hero there.
The ruffian band, o'erawed, dismayed,
The mandate stern, at once obeyed;
On me his piercing glances fell,
Who, here, this soldier's rank can tell?
My old tormentor broke again,
Great Knight of Night-caps, Barren Brain!
He struck the speaker with his sword,
But with the flat: another word,
Foul jester, and to thee I serve
The felon doom, you well deserve.
Milbank—mute, trembling, turned aside,
As from the stranger's gaze to hide;
But with stern word, and piercing glance,
He bade him publish forth at once,
My rank and name. With down cast eye,
He spoke—Sir Arthur's orderly,
Known in the ranks as Shane O'Neill.
And who art thou? At this appeal,
Like aspen leaf my comrade shook,
Dismay oppressed his downcast look,
His palsied tongue refused to tell;
I felt my heart with pity swell.
'Tis Milbank, drummer in the band,
Arrested by St. Clair's command,
I made reply; and doomed to mourn,
In durance, till St. Clair's return.
If e'er he come, a sadder lot,
The wretched man will then be shot.
Ah! ruffian Milbank, I proclaim

An instant doom, with deeper shame ;
Foul murderer ! a felon's doom,
Will be thy herald to the tomb.
Prepare to meet thy damning fate,
Prepare thy guilt to expiate ;
Prepare thy soul, thy race is run,
Thou murderer of the widow's son :
See his avenger—Marion.
Beg Heaven's forgiveness, bend the knee,
Thou'lt hang upon the nearest tree.
Inhuman monster ! mother earth,
That you've polluted since your birth,
Now spurns you from her injured breast,
Denies your reeking vileness rest ;
Denies thy carcass couch of clay,
And leaves thee naked, to decay—
Where hungry vultures, fierce and lean,
May batten on your flesh unclean.
Milbank had fallen flat with fear,
Foul birds of kin, take him from here,
Swing him aloft, 'twixt earth and sky,
I'll view, myself, the villain die.
Thou, Mickey Free, and scarce less vile,
Art hangman—wake a jest or smile,
Or word, from all thy villain crew,
Of levity, by all that's true
And sacred, thou shalt get thy due.
Bear the offensive brute away,
Five minutes will suffice to pray ;
Then hang the wolf. By very force
They bore him—like a helpless corse ;

Heart sick, I turned my head away,
My watch upon my pillow lay;
But by what power, or magic spell,
To me restored, I ne'er could tell.
Soon as the work of death was done,
Returned alone, bold Marion ;
And said by fortunes fitful scale,
Thou art a prisoner here, O'Neill,
And subject to each let and bar,
Of callous unrelenting war.
Pledge me a soldier's honor fair,
That thou will not from hence repair,
Nor ought, that you may hap to know,
Would vantage give my country's foe
You tell, till thou hast my command,
Or peace has blest our harrass'd land ;
This ratify, and on parole,
When health permits without control,
You wander free, within such bounds,
As circle of a mile surrounds;
The centre here. I blessed the boon,
And ratified the pledge full soon.
One hundred pounds the promised prize,
Is thine : This paper certifies
The ruffians end, and by whose aid
Came retribution long delayed.
That youth, a widowed mother's pride,
Where Marion went was by his side,
On peril's path, on toilsome ride,
Death only did our course divide ;
By strategy decoyed—betrayed

To cruel death—unfit to aid,
And left for dead, his comrade saw
Milbank, his ruffian dagger draw,
And in the life blood foully spilt,
Lave his vile hands, oh! deed of guilt:
Such was his wounded comrade's tale,
Alas, to late came Shane O'Neill,
The orderly of stern St. Clair,
And poured the balm of mercy there;
But all too late: death's dread eclipse,
Had sealed for aye those truthful lips.
He grasped my hand, yes, comrade brave,
You gave my boy a soldier's grave,
The desclate, the deed shall know,
A deed heroic in a foe;
And heaven who hears that mother's wail,
Will thee reward, Adieu O'Neill.
Ere I could speak, he fled the place,
I never since beheld his face;
But owned his bounty, shared his care,
Mid scenes that else had wrought despair.
Kind friends, the soldier softly cries,
My tedious tale, thy patience tries,
But I approach its welcome close,
How on the ship my quarrel rose,
My latest peril, by the aid,
Of my young comrade well portrayed.
Oh! had the veteran scann'd each maid,
Or gazed upon the Matron's face,
Where tears, like rain drops flowed a pace,
Those heart's pure tribute, bright and warm,

14

Might well his idle fears disarm.
At last fond peace with angel wand,
Brought blessings to the bleeding land,
Wept o'er the brave—immortal now,
Wreathed chaplets for the victor's brow,
And poured sweet balm the wounds to heal,
Wrought by war's rugged hand of steel;
And England's last and shattered band,
Bade farewell to the rescued land;
My self among the reckless few,
That latest bade the shores adieu:
But now compelled by cruel fate,
With fiends in human shape, to mate;
Who, when the soul so much in need,
Of heavenly aid, for aid would plead;
My breast was wounded with foul cry
Of mocking jest, and blasphemy:
Now common sport of lawless rule,
Called black O'Neill, through ridicule;
Till on that day, these hounds of hell,
Their former orgies far excell,
Decking an image meant to scorn,
The Mother, by whom Christ was born!
Mock worshippers with tongues unclean,
Intoned a psalmody obscene;
By well laid plans, myself beguiled,
My ears were with the sounds defiled,
But when I learned the import drear,
'Twas more than Christian flesh could bear.
I felled the foremost with my hand,
And trampling o'er the prostrate band;

Tore from its place the effigy,
And blood besmeared the living lie,
And stained my hands ; a saber lay
At hand, with which I forced my way
Among my foes ; 'till sorely prest,
I gained the deck ; you know the rest.
Kind friends, if yet a soldier's tale,
Has not removed the mystic veil,
That wed my name with Shane O'Neill ;
Still other proofs I may explore :
They all reply, we ask no more.
And on that swart and rugged face,
Each 'gan some comeliness to trace ;
Foot prints, tho' faint, of former grace.
The shepherd bard now joins the band,
O'Donnel grasps his proffered hand,
The grateful soldier's rough address,
And hearty grasp his thanks express :
Saved by thy courage, strength and skill,
Mid unseen perils of the hill,
Where I, all helpless made my lair,
You staked your life to reach me there,
You pitying heaven's auxilary,
Without whose aid I soon must die ;
Long may your manly bosom glow,
In triumph over every foe,
Temptation, trial, hazard pain,
If these assail, may thou sustain,
Each dread assault, the victor still
O'er self, and every lesser ill.
To this brave youth my life I owe,

And here my grateful thanks bestow.
Such praise, the shepherd blushed to hear,
But sweet it fell on Ellen's ear,
And deep within her partial breast,
She treasured all; and mutely blessed,
The rugged lips, that thus approve
Her heart's dear idol—such is love.
The youthful guest unsheathed the sword,
And o'er the glittering legend por'd
In silence: from the record there,
Read, " Arthur Bolingbroke St. Clair.
To Hugh O'Donnel, once his foe.
Right worthy son of great Hugh Roe,
In thy true hand, this virgin blade,
Will shield the weak, the helpless aid,
The right defend, the wrong oppose,
Till justice triumphs o'er her foes;
And joy, and peace, and freedom smile,
On lovely Erin's faithful isle;
Go! scion of a princely tree,
Fair type of true nobility,
Thy ancestor's renown, restore
Back to thy native Goreymore."
Whilst thus he read the legend's close,
His swelling breast with care o'er flows,
Dark shadows former joy control,
And sad misgivings fill his soul;
Comrade, he cried! is he whose praise,
Shines in the legend's golden blaze,
On this true blade's unsullied steel;
Is he alive, in woe or weal?

Does home's sweet sanctity once more,
The wanderer bless by Goreymore;
Or victim of a victor band,
Fills he a grave in foreign land?
He was my friend; art thou his mate?
I hold his brand, declare his fate.
That speech, like sudden thunder-stroke;
The soldier's sterner mien awoke,
He started, instant from his chair,
And on the stripling fixed his glare;
Anger, resentment, rage amaze!
Like lightning from his eye balls blaze,
And like that fatal dread repose,
The serpent round his victim throws;
Matron and maids spell-bound arise,
Attracted by those flashing eyes.
First! rash inquisitor, proclaim!
The soldier harshly spoke, thy name.
With instant speech the youth replies,
Defiance flashing from his eyes,
Companions' tongues too partial still,
Named me the boy of Bunker Hill.
The soldier from the youth withdrew,
Those fiercer rays that looked him thro',
With milder mien, but steadfast gaze,
From head to foot the youth surveys;
Oh! dull of heart, he cried, and smiled,
It is my fair heroic child,
His gallant form, his comely face,
He op'ed his arms in fond embrace;
Back from his reach the youth recoiled,

Avaunt! dread man, thy guile is foiled,
Base counterfeit, back I command!
Or feel the vengence of this brand.
The angry steel in light displayed,
The soldier saw and stood dismayed:
Then farther from the youth withdrew;
Veiled with both hands his face from view,
His giant breast like billows high
In tempest, heaved in agony;
And tears, like summer's sudden rain,
That face of bronze suffused amain,
Till hearts, so late by terror swayed,
With tears, a pitying tribute paid.
Like dew drops on the fragrant rose,
The tender tear that sweetly flows,
From lovely woman's pitying eye,
And sweetly fragrant her soft sigh;
As that pure incense borne around,
On summer gales, where blooms abound.
But man, stern man, by nature rude,
His fiercer soul with fire imbued;
His breast encased in stubborn mail,
His sigh, sounds like the tempest's wail,
When mighty ships in ruin cast,
Lie stranded by the ruthless blast;
And manhood's tears, if tears he shed,
Like wave of fire on Hecla's head,
Gush up in furious fitful throws
To war, with his eternal snows.
Such war of nature here behold,
In this stern man by grief controll'd;
He mutters in his wretched need,

Oh ! this is misery indeed.
Is the proud oak so sadly riven,
So blasted by the bolts of heaven?
That those fair vines that round it sprung,
And 'mong its foliage twined and clung,
And owned its summer's sheltering stay,
Turn from the leafless trunk away;
He raised his hands that veiled his face,
My erring child, seest thou no trace,
No record, be it e'er so slight;
No ray undimmed, of former light?
Scan these warped features once again,
In mercy scan. Bold man ! in vain
You urge vile strategy, as well
Call darkness light; not heaven to hell,
So much unlike as he you try,
To counterfeit; thou living lie.
The soldier flung his vest away,
And knelt him down as if to pray;
The inner garment that he wore,
Back from his swelling bosom tore,
Bright in the sunbeam's parting glow,
That bosom shone, and white as snow,
And fair portrayed with varied dye,
The sacred scene of Calvary.
The holy cross raised on the hill,
The Savior crowned, and bleeding still ;
The Mother whelm'd in woe profound,
Her soul in deepest anguish drown'd,
And Magdalen, her arms around
The sacred wood, in sorrow's sea,
Immersed, clings to the hallowed tree.

A wreath of Shamrocks traced with skill,
Seems clinging to the rugged hill;
Within its circle fair to view,
Was writ in letters red and blue,
Hugh Roe O'Donnel of the glen,
In holy faith of Christ, Amen.
Bear witness heaven, I speak the truth,
The soldier cried, strike ardent youth,
In mercy strike, oh why delay,
Behold! I turn my head away,
Yea, from thy gaze my soul disguise,
The gates are shut: he closed his eyes,
The setting sun in warm farewell,
Against that swarthy visage fell;
And on the whitewashed wall in view,
A well proportioned portrait threw;
Where lines of beauty, curves of grace,
All harmonize without one trace,
Of rude relentless blighting war,
Its manly comeliness to mar;
Struck by that picture on the wall,
The youth his naked brand let fall;
For in that graceful shadowed head,
He sees a spectre from the dead.
The gentle Mary standing near,
The kneeling man, and pale with fear;
First on his rayless visage gazed,
Then on his heaving breast: Amazed,
She scanned each scene of sacred woe,
Explored the circling wreath below,
Oh bliss of bliss, where hope was none;
That seal has recognition won.

Silent, as falls the modest beam,
Of night's fair queen on troubled stream;
Changing its turbid restless flow,
To silver wave's refulgent glow;
On that vexed bosom sank the maid;
On his rough cheek her own she laid;
My father, Oh! my father dear,
Broke on the soldier's startled ear;
Instinctive closed the father's arms,
Around his daughter's faultless charms;
Her gushing tears of tender joy
Commingling with the dark alloy,
Of anguished breast's up-welling woe,
Bid wave from brighter fountain flow;
He feels her breath, a scented gale,
And warm—his sunburnt cheek assail;
He hears her sobs of rapture start,
Marks each pulsation of her heart,
Entranced, bewildered, motionless,
He fears it all a dream of bliss;
Till Mary, gazing in his eyes,
Fond memory's missing link supplies,
And in the maiden's matchless grace,
Beholds sweet childhood's angel face,
Of every darksome doubt beguiled;
He cries, my own my darling child:
Treasure of treasures, hope and pride.
Thus closed on rude Glentogher's side,
Our tale at holy Christmas tide.

END OF THIRD CANTO.

THE FRIAR'S CURSE—CANTO FOURTH.

Dear to the muse when uncontroll'd,
'Mid wild Glentogher's mountain hold,
Stern winter, with his stubborn train
Of followers, riots in his reign;
Pouring in reckless sport his wrath,
Round 'lated traveler's wildered path,
Who worn and weak on Cloghan high,
Beholds the storm-king's revelry.
Dear then to her at close of day,
To steal to mountain cot away;
To list the legends travelers tell,
Who wildered in the mountain dell,
Find shelter in the peasant's home.
Yet dearer still, when she can roam,
Like butterfly, from flower to flower,
When summer mild, with magic power,
Her scepter sways, and dell and grove,
Ring vocal with the voice of love;
And Fairy Glens, whose vesture sheen,
Of velvet moss and ivy green,
With fragrant Primrose soft and bright,
Refulgent glows: 'tis her delight,
To wander with the balmy breeze,
On fairy wings, 'neath shady trees;
To list the tales that lovers tell,

By babbling stream, by grove and dell,
To hear the lark who warbles long,
In azure sky his matchless song;
Whilst from the thicket by the lake,
Black-bird and thrush their notes awake.
Oh summer's smile of joy for me,
For then indeed the Muse is free.
And where in all the world beside,
A land that woo's so fair a tide,
As thine Strabreagy, or a sea,
Mirrors, such magic scenery;
Green vales and fertile slopes, and grand
Old mountains tower'ng o'er the strand,
Forest and glade, a Fairy land,
Magnificently wild and gay.
[1]And matchless all. But Oraray,
Thy vale in summer verdure drest,
To my—perhaps too partial breast,
Transcends in beauty, chaste serene,
And reigns o'er all the landscape—Queen.
Dear Oraray whose green-wood bowers,
Have often claimed my truant hours,
Whose laurels bright, and chestnuts green,
The wild, the wayward boy, did screen,
When oft he stole at close of day,
Whilst dew-drops hung like silver spray
On leaf and blow. In lonely dell,
Youth's rosy dream of love to tell
To trusting innocence; and steal
Sweet balm for wounds he would not heal;
Or, thro' some shaded track pursue,

Alone, the muse he loved to woo ;
The lowly muse, she comes once more,
To wander by thy matchless shore,
An outcast from her native wild,
A prodigal, a spendthrift child ;
Long exiled from a mother's care,
Where fortune flees her baffled heir ;
Yet thou hast never been forgot,
By thy rude child, dear natal spot.
With filial love fond fairy land,
She comes to wander o'er thy strand.
Thy strand whose lucid summer wave,
Did oft my youthful bosom lave ;
Whose every mountain—glen and rill,
And blue-bell bank, and heath brown hill,
Fresh round my memory cluster still,
And loved, as when in early years,
I wandered there with my compeers.
My fond compeers, the fair and gay,
The bold, the gentle, where are they ?
In every clime beneath the sun :
A friendly fate, ere well begun
The race of life, bade some find rest,
Reclining on their mother's breast ;
Some on the field of crimsoned strife,
Glory their prize, gave up their life ;
By woe and want some stricken down,
Now wear in bliss, the martyr's crown ;
And some like me are struggling still,
'Gainst tide and time, with stubborn will
The sands are low, and fierce the wave,

May victory crown the struggling brave.
For me—the muse with kindly smile,
From contest rude, shall me beguile
To childhood's scenes, where fancy fair,
May still her airy structures rear ;
Sweet scenes of childhood, oh, how true,
Fond memory brings you back to view.
[2]Thy haunted Hawthorn by the sea
Unfolds its fragrant bloom to me,
Its ripening blows, like wreaths of snow,
Are floating on the wave below ;
I see the timid stripling gaze
In awe, as I in childhood's days,
Lest Faries work his spell of doom,
Crossing their track in twilight's gloom ;
Once more thy sainted hermit's cell,
I seek, and own that hallowed spell,
That heavenly love doth still bestow,
Where virtue sanctified below.
Here oft in childhood's guileless day,
I've crossed my breast, and knelt to pray ;
Such was the tributary toll,
Old legends say his parting soul
Desired : Who enters this rude shed,
Prays for that holy hermit—dead.
Oh, human heart, oh, heart of mine,
If he, whose life long virtues shine
Refulgent as the stainless snow,
Own such uncertainty to go
Down that dark road, that unknown bourne,
Whence traveler ne'er did back return ;

Oh! what a crushing anguish pile
Awaits the soul of sin and guile
On that dim shore, that bounds thy sea,
Unfathomed dread eternity:
Saints, from the quicksands succor me,
And sinners all. Again I rove,
By rude Drumcroy's Badger Cove,
And thorny braes, where oft I strayed,
A truant rogue, when others prayed;
Ah! little dreamt a father then,
How oft I lingered in that glen,
With my compeers, as wild and gay,
And graceless, laggarts on the way
To shrines of prayer—advent'rous bold,
Some stormed the Jackdaw's airy hold,
Whilst some below, with ruthless hand,
Despoiled poor pusses' house of sand.
And oft like pirates o'er their prey,
Fierce contests closed our lawless day;
And last—remorse our souls inspire,
For each must brave a Father's ire;
Oh! rest that honored name in grace,
And thanks to heaven, tho' rash my race,
And reckless oft, more prized than gold,
More dear than life, that faith so old,
Shrined in my heart—its hopes I hold.
Thrice welcome ancient Goreymore;
Thou lovliest wild of all that shore,
With joy I scan that castle high,
Crowned with the ivied canopy;
Whilst woodbine tapstry bright and gay,

The porch adorns ; full many a day,
Have I usurped proud Oughie's throne ;
[3]Great Fairy King of Inishowen,
And t'aen my comrades young to beat,
In boyish bold advent'rous feat,
Possession of the royal seat;
Yet trembling, lest some wicked sprite,
With Elfin stone my reign would blight.
Oh dear, I love thy monarch's hold,
Thy spreading shades, and bosom bold,
Fair Goreymore. Each crag and dell,
That threw o'er early years its spell,
And those grand Monarch Hills that rise,
In pride, and pierce my native skies ;
Sky, hill and plain, so calm and clear,
Within Strabreagy's wave appear,
Seem fairy land, so soft and true,
The lovely lake reflects the view.
Give o'er fond heart reflections vain :
Wake, wandering muse thy tale again.

TALE.

The summer sun's unclouded ray,
Had dried the dew drops' silver spray,
That hung at dawn of morn, on flower
And leaf, in Gorey's haunted bower ;
Save, where 'neath deep and denser screen,
Of wilderness of foliage sheen,
On primrose tuft and blue bell's breast,

Unseen, the pearly sleepers rest;
Still in the brake the Mavis sung,
His Matins, for the day was young;
When by old Gorey's runlet's brink,
A youthful traveler stooped to drink,
His thirst allayed, he bends him low,
'Til o'er his brow the waters flow,
Then from his dark locks flung the spray,
And westward urged again his way.
That slender form of youth and grace,
The smile that lights his sun-brown'd face,
His step of pride, and bearing bold,
Tho' other guise his limbs enfold;
And summer garments wrap his breast,
Proclaim to us, our youthful guest,
Who, snow-bound on Glentogher's side,
We left at holy Christmas tide.
What, tho' these tempting shades invite,
To soft repose the wandering wight;
What tho' he looks with wistful eye,
As if some refuge to descry:
Oft peers beneath the thicket's screen,
He passes by the lovely scene,
Yet often turns again to gaze,
Back on old Gorey's hazel braes.
Where Balagh's wandering waters glide,
Commingling with Strabreagy's tide;
He shuns the lakelet's pebbly strand,
And threads a dell 'twixt hills of sand,
Where blinding drift, and trackless way,
His weary footsteps long delay;

Then gaining Cranny's basement broad,
He climbs the steep, but firmer road,
That leads where troubled nature's war,
Flung Cranny's granite gates ajar,
And to the plane beyond, a pass
Op'ed thro' the adamantine mass;
Here to the left, against the sky,
A splintered column shoots on high,
Like watch tower by some giant's hold,
Whose peak a boundless view controll'd
From that grey cliff our hero gazed,
Enrapt, delighted and amazed:
For in that rugged northern land,
No scene so charming, lovely, grand.
The boundless ocean's billows roll'd,
Beneath his throne, at depth untold.
And ceaseless beat with mighty shock,
'Gainst lone Glasshedy's island rock,
Then sweeping to the mainland shore,
Sank on the beach with sullen roar,
Draping each other's funeral pall,
With robes of snow to mark their fall.
Beyond the breakers—gloomy, grand,
Huge Knockamany's barriers stand:
Grim guardsman, black with strife and age,
He laughs to scorn the ocean's rage.
There fair Knockglass, like gentle Queen,
Bedecked in robes of richest green,
In majesty enthroned—beside
Her rugged consort's gloomy pride,
She stoops religion's shrine to greet

15*

That lowly nestles at her feet,
And keeps unwearied watch and ward,
O'er Chapel old, and lone Churchyard.
Calm vale and brooklet intervene,
Till lofty Cranny bounds the scene.
Far westward as the eye may strain,
Old Torry rises from the Main—
A snowy cloud in azure sky,
Unchanged it hangs, you wonder why.
A narrow inlet ope's the way,
To fair Strabreagy's sheltered bay.
But cones of sand unnumbered rise,
And from the view the strait disguise.
Yon ruined tower, whose blackened pile,
Looms o'er the beach on Doah's isle,
Seen thro' the ocean's misty spray,
At times it seems to melt away;
Then bursting into light and form,
It frowns defiance on the storm,
Still eastward, cast in softer mould,
Strabreagy's matchless shores unfold,
Grove, Mountain, Hamlet, Lake and Plain;
Ah, me! description were in vain,
Go view them from our hero's stand,
And own, you've looked on Fairyland,
Such were the scenes, fair, rude and wild,
That long the stranger's stay beguiled,
Till swayed by lonely solitude,
Sad musings on his soul intrude,
Whilst on yon towering cliff he stands,
And shades his vision with his hands;

Now gazes up the mountain high,
Now down the slope, now on the sky,
O'er ocean's wave above below,
Whilst thus, his words spontaneous flow,
And of his pensive musings show.

I

See how those angry vapors fly
In wild career, like mountain streams,
Athwart the Day-God's track on high,
And steal from earth his golden beams;
Those clouds that shed a chilling gloom,
To liquid air will melt away,
And beams of joy will yet illume
The laughing land, 'ere close of day.

II.

Behold! upon the ocean's breast,
The billows rushing to the shore,
Whilst foam and mist float on their crest,
They greet the rocks with sullen roar;
Mild zephyrs soon will lull to sleep,
This boist'rous breeze that jarring sound,
And peace allay the troubled deep,
Where foam clad billows now abound.

III.

But oh, my heart whose morning light,
With hope all warm, was drowned in care;
Wilt thou regain youth's radiance bright,
Shall peace and bliss to thee repair,

Must gloom and sadness hover nigh,
The soul bereft of youthful rest,
Will gentle airs ne'er lull the sigh,
That wakes thy billows—weary breast?
He dried the tear that dimmed his eye,
Descended from his eyrie high;
Now scans the rugged narrow way,
Whose mazy windings downward stray,
And o'er the valley's verdant sod,
Lead to yon humble House of God;
Lowly the walls, the Altar rude,
No solemn pomps its porch intrude.
No blessed bell with silver chime,
Wakes matin's hour, tells vesper's time,
Nor organ's swelling voice sounds there;
But hearts as pure, have knelt in prayer,
On thy cold floor of flowing sand,
Thou lowliest Temple in the land,
Dear Lag, as in the marbled aisle,
Of Great Saint Peter's matchless pile.
Nay, fear not stranger youth to go,
Adown that path to vale below,
Tho' steep and rude, the softest maid,
From Drung to Ballagh's not afraid,
To press the daisies that array
The margin of the mazy way.
Ah! reckless stranger thou shalt rue,
If thou, that upward track pursue,
It leads o'er Cranny's wildest keep,
To way so difficult and steep;
Its herbage sweet, the mountain sheep

May never crop. Then stay! oh, stay
Thy steps, and seek the safer way.
Behold him! rashly move along,
The dizzy height: well brace thee strong;
Thy heart and limb, advent'rer young,
One foot misplaced, and thou art flung
From Cranny's breast, far, far below,
A feast for yonder carrion crow.
That fearful track on Cranny's side,
Ne'er traced by stranger lacking guide,
Is by the dauntless stripling prest,
As he were nurtured on its breast;
Safe, sinks he in the torrent's bed,
Unscathed, regains his airy tread,
The shelving rock the torrent scar,
His path oppose, but may not bar,
Till far projecting sharp and bold,
In angle of the mountain hold
A crag abruptly juts before,
And blocks the way, a mountain o'er
His wildered head, that not a goat
Would dare to climb, below a moat
So steep and deep, the sable crow,
That wings its flight half way below
No larger meets the climber's ken,
Who dares the view, than mountain wren,
Well, may he ponder here and pause,
O'er dark destruction's gaping jaws;
He wipes the moisture from his brow,
And stays his foot. Upreaching now,
His hand, a stunted bush would grasp,

High, higher still, it meets his clasp,
On Heaven, and on that bush depends
Thy life, one look above he sends,
Now hugs the cliff, now swings in air;
Adventerous youth, no loving fair,
Meets thy embrace, yet to thy breast,
Thou ne'er hast maiden closer prest,
Then this grey Crag—for life or death,
He toils and struggles, till his breath
And strength exhausted; motionless
He hangs above the dread abbyss.
Now youth thy rash adventure mourn,
Vain act, thou canst not back return,
Nor hope for human hands to aid;
To desperate chance thy life's betrayed.
One effort fails, one struggle more,
A space above his bosom bore;
And there to ease his panting breast;
The danger past, he lay at rest.
'Twere long to trace his farther way,
Down Cranny's steep, that summer's day,
And o'er the mazy path that led,
To Lag's lone dwelling of the dead,
Where many a moss-grown tablet found
Half buried in its ruined mound,
And bones that bleaching lie around,
Proclaim the place, long hallowed ground;
Yet ere he crossed the threshold o'er,
Of that old churchyard's lowly door,
The symbol where a saviour bled,
Looked down on his uncovered head.

And when with noiseless step, he prest
The sod that wraps each sleeper's breast,
He breathed a prayer—Oh, cheering faith,
For souls, whose hearts lie still beneath.
Oh! wond'rous sleep, that knows no waking,
Till the eternal day-beam breaking;
Oh glorious day! oh, day of dread,
That breaks the slumbers of the dead;
At last he paused, where sweetly wave,
Wild blossoms o'er an humble grave,
Whose shamrock sod, and mountain rose,
That o'er the sleeper's bosom blows,
Bespeak long undisturbed repose;
Nor cross, nor emblem sculptured fair,
Gives record of the sleeper there;
Yet incense sweet, by blue-bells shed,
By filial love, or friendship spread
In wild profusion, mutely tells,
In some true heart the record dwells;
A while in doubt he gazed around,
Then knelt beside the lowly mound,
Tho' flowers lie spread by hand unknown,
And gone, the monumental stone,
His heart's instinctive fountains flow,
In tears, for one who sleeps below;
But hark! what fearful crash assails,
And who so loud and wildly wails.
Yon roofless ruin's broken wall,
Some mourner crushes in its fall,
See, sand and dust in volume high,
Now climb above, and shroud the sky,

As Dundeer swift as mountain stream,
Impetuous—to the rescue came
The stranger youth; his earnest will
Urging to shield from further ill,
Above that wretched form in fear,
He curbed at once his proud career,
As if he saw a chasm below,
Where soul unshriven told its woe.
Nor mortal seems, that fleshless hand,
Upraised 'mong clouds of dust and sand;
Nor wears that form, an earthly mein,
Now hidden quite, now dimly seen,
As denser sinks the dusty shroud,
Or bouyant soars, the lighter cloud,
That upward high, and higher borne,
Lets sunbeams light a face forlorn,
From whose blear'd eyes, the tear drops leap,
And trace long channels dark and deep
Down her soiled features, till they wear,
The lineaments of wild despair;
Mid wreck of masonry she stands,
Clapping in agony her hands,
Her form bowed down by age or woe,
And quivering strong, rocks to and fro,
Keeping in measured motion, time
With her loud wail's spontaneous rhyme:
A slate with strange uncouth device,
Low at her feet, and shattered, lies,
O'er this she makes her weary moan,
Washing with tears the ruined stone;
Full on the breeze, like banner spread,

Floats her soiled cloak of Tyrian red,
Her hood forsakes her hoary head,
And wildly on the ruthless blast,
Her scanty tresses grey are cast,
Whilst rising with the rising gale,
The air is vocal with her wail.

WAIL.

I.

Like the promise that met her,
'Tis blighted and broken ;
The fate that beset her
Now clings to this token;
Like her bosom, 'tis shattered
By true love's intrusion,
Like her hopes crushed and scattered
In ruin's confusion.

II.

Nor kindred, nor brother
Stood near her when dying ;
In the grave of another,
My love light is lying;
In emblem is spoken,
Her house's sad story ;
Its 'scutcheon thus broken,
Tells the wreck of its glory.

16

III.

Thou crest of the mighty,
  Time was, if in danger,
Bold bosoms would right thee ;
  A woman, a stranger—
Heart broken and lonely,
  Misfortune pursuing,
Now weeps for thee only,
  Now weeps o'er thy ruin.

IV.

Ah ! where is the treasure
  Once placed in my keeping,
Tears come without measure
  The absent one weeping,
The ocean is flowing,
  To sunder us ever,
Unknown and unknowing :
  Ah ! why did we sever ?

High on the broken battlement,
The stranger heard the wild lament,
And deemed, that being wailing there,
A soul unblest, and in despair,
Or boding Banshe come to tell,
The prelude to his funeral knell ;
Cold dew drops from his temples start,
And life's pent current chills his heart;
Quiver his bloodless lips with pain,
And twice essay to speak, in vain,

And pale as marble shines his brow:
At last he utters, who art thou?
Startled her bony hands, she raised
To free her sight, and wildly gazed
Above her, where the stranger stood,
Intruder on her solitude:
O'er form and face her vision ran,
Then answered, I am Hannah Bawn.
My own fond foster Mother, she
Whom I deemed dead, ah! do I see,
Her living form? Then mother dear,
Behold! thy long lost Edmond here.
He comes to shield thy tottering age,
He comes, thy sorrows to assuage,
He comes to cheer life's wintry day,
And part of childhood's debt repay;
He leaped below by love controlled,
To aid that pilgrim weird and old.
Back! base intruder, back, she cries!
With fire indignant flash her eyes,
Nor mock a lonely woman's woe,
Back, else I fell thee with a blow
Of this rough rock whose harshest part,
Owns more of human than thy heart;
She grasped the stone with frenzied eye,
And form erect, now mocker fly,
Leave crazy Hannah here alone,
In solitude, to make her moan;
Or rue thy wanton sport, and tread
Unholy, o'er the sacred dead,
Whose bleaching bones, and hallowed clay,

Thy presence spurn, hell-hound away!
She swung the missile round and round,
But Edmond still maintained his ground,
Full well he knew that tender breast,
In courage fierce, so falsely drest,
To save herself from wrong or harm,
Would shrink to tread the lowly worm;
She dropped the missile where she stood,
And thus resumed in calmer mood,
Oh! reckless stranger why so rude?
Why trifle thus with Hannah's care?
He, whom I mourned, his brow was fair,
Rosy his cheeks, his flaxen hair,
Hung round his neck in ringlets wild;
Mother! I was that comely child,
Fierce suns, and fiercer scenes have changed,
My once bright brow, my heart estranged,
To soon from childhood's sweet repose,
Stole from the wanderer's cheek, the rose;
And years of trial, trust and care,
Have dyed my locks that once were fair;
Tho' changed in looks, oh! mother, see,
I have not changed in love to thee.
The youth approached, but doubt and fear,
In Hannah's troubled look appear;
His form and voice, alike unknown,
She cannot trust that tender tone,
That thrills her heart, she waves her hand,
Approach not stranger, I command!
Then from amid the ruin crept,
And on a tombstone sat and wept,

Sad sobs in Edmond's bosom rise,
And big tears trickle from his eyes ;
Oh ! must the orphan plead in vain,
And mourn fond memory's broken chain;
That chain of love, whose sundered parts,
Are treasured by our wounded hearts ;
Oh ! gaze on this, thou know'st the best,
To whom belongs that curious crest,
You gave it Edmond, 'twas you said,
Ta'en from a mother's finger—dead ;
Oh ! let that sacred emblem chide
The heart, that my embrace denied :
She gained her feet, tho' bowed with grief,
And trembling like an aspen leaf,
In summer's sigh. More close she pressed
Her cross and beads against her breast;
Approached the youth, and closely scann'd
His face, then viewed his outstretched hand.
As leaps the landscape into light,
When meteor bursts on blackest night;
One ray from that long treasured crest,
Remembrance kindled in her breast,
She threw her arms aloft, and wild
Exclaimed, 'tis he, my wand'ring child,
But blisses' gushing torrent tide,
Old Hannah's further speech denied,
Whilst Edmond's arms around her thrown,
Press her old bosom to his own.
Oh love, how cold our speech would be,
Were our rude language reft of thee,
Of words, thou great divinity ;

What fond emotion rules the breast,
That is not all by thee expressed,
Emotions, various as the hue
Of flowers that bathe in summer's dew,
And fragrant pure, as that perfume,
That hovers round the rose's bloom.
'Tis thine to name the mystic vine,
Whose tendrils round young hearts entwine;
Or torn by fate, or friends apart,
Still closer bind each bleeding heart;
But all in vain will love express,
Or gratitude, that tenderness,
That burning unconsuming flame,
In Edmond's breast, it has no name;
But faith's mild eye, with vision true,
Sees angels in the azure blue,
Wafting to love divine on high,
Each tear that 'scapes his moistened eye.
And angel tongues aloud proclaim
In Heaven, that holiest passion's name.
O'er that old breast, its treasures flow,
Till age forgets its load of woe
So sweet the wave; and long she drank,
Till all exhausted on the bank,
With joys excess, old Hannah sank.
Oh! human heart, strange citadel,
Where bliss and woe, where passions fell,
And virtues rare, contending dwell;
Heaven born humility with pride
Dread foe of peace, to hell allied,
From reason's earliest dawn, till age

His shadow spreads, in strife engage:
Here joy, like sunshine in the glade,
Smiles bright and warm, in ambuscade,
Sits sorrow, brooding in the shade
In sleepless watch, prepared to smite,
With ruthless hand, the seraph bright.
A breath, and bliss her form reveals,
Still sorrow's sable Angel steals
So close, she treads the seraph's heels;
Thus Hannah's heart o'erflowed with joy,
When fate restored her orphan boy;
As long neglected memories rise,
Grief seeks the shrine in fond disguise,
And curbing joy's too blissful reign,
Usurps by guile the fair domain.
Unfailing aid had Hannah still,
Her balm in woe, her shield in ill;
She knelt her down in silent prayer,
To Heaven unfolded all her care,
Then by the youth resumed her place,
And thanks our Lady—Queen of Grace,
Gazing on Edmond's thoughtful face.
Blessed thy name, oh! spotless Maid,
The orphan's guide, the sinner's aid,
Who, with a mother's tender care,
Receives the child's imperfect prayer,
That clogged with selfish love and pride,
And born in sin, had vainly sighed,
At heaven's unyielding barrier fair,
For naught impure may enter there;
Had'st thou not glean'd the brighter part,

From the wild chaos of the heart,
And borne on lips immaculate,
To glorious heaven's unfolding gate,
Where ministers at mercy's throne
Present the offering all thy own.
Oh! Edmond dear, when dark and low,
My weary heart was bow'd with woe,
That name, of names the first the best,
Invoked, restores the soul to rest.
Then Mary's mild protection seek
Whilst youth and vigor flush thy cheek,
And fortune smiles with look benign,
Fortune and bloom, and youth were mine;
As melts the snow in summer's ray,
These gifts as faithless, pass away;
But Mary's love in fulness teems,
When fortune frowning folds her beams,
As stars, in glory beam by night,
But veil their rays when all is bright.
'Twas Mary's love and succor mild,
Thy mother cheer'd mid trials wild,
That else had crushed in dark despair
Her broken heart; whose morning fair,
Beaming with promise, warm and bright,
In darkest eclipse sank ere night:
Love, heart and hope in ruin laid,
She meekly bore with Mary's aid.
And on that night, whose sore distress,
Thyself unborn, left fatherless;
When o'er our heads in fury fell,
The angry billow's mountain swell,

And five brave men, and young as brave,
Engulfed in one cold watery grave.
Tho' sudden and untimley sped,
The bolt, whose dreadful thunder said,
Arise! oh soul, shake off thy dust!
A judge, avenging, jealous, just,
A God who gave, demands the trust:
'Tis sweet to know thy father's breath,
Tho' struggling in the toils of death,
His loving Saviour's pardon sued,
And Mary's intercession woo'd.
Awhile in silent sorrow bound,
His tearful eyes fixed on the ground;
Edmond sat pensive, pondering o'er
A father's fate, unknown before;
Then spoke, my guide and guardian still,
My parent's trust, thro' good and ill,
Thou, who their hopes and hardships shar'd,
Whom Heaven, in tender mercy spar'd,
To share their orphan's sore distress,
And succor childhood's helplessness;
To me—their lives unknown—portray,
And tell me of their spring time day.
Edmond's imploring tone and look,
His old companion ill could brook;
She rose, and turning cast her glance,
O'er troubled ocean's broad expanse,
On ruined hulk and shattered spar,
Of wrecks, that strewed Strabreagy's bar,
From island rock to frowing ben,
From beach to billow glanced her ken:

Till black and grim the turrets old,
On Doah's isle, her gaze controll'd.
So would the painter's vision stray,
So would the muse the scene survey,
Till from the wond'rous wild around,
The soul, her inspiration found.
With moan that told her anguish drear,
She clasp'd her hands and cried, 'twas there.
That instant, pent up grief awoke,
And from her stricken bosom broke:
O'er ocean's roar above the gale;
Old Cranny's echoes spoke the wail,
And knockamenny's barrier high,
And distant, hoarse returns the cry;
Till grieving at her grief's excess,
She fled the place in sore distress,
And on the rude mound, lately prest
By him who follows, flung her breast;
Here incoherent, wild and rude,
Her sobs and wail awhile intrude,
Then plaintive as the bittern's cry,
And free as lark in summer's sky,
At times scarce heard, now slow, now fast,
As o'er her mind, the vision passed,
Whilst flows her heart's emotion strong,
Her lips awake spontaneous song.

KEENA

The sunbeams bright, in floods of light,
  Gild blue-hill's bosom fair;
And wilding Rose, and fragrant blows,
  Exhale sweet incense there;
The Robin alone from his airy throne
  On the old oak, whistles shrill,
And a hundred throats wake their wildwood notes
  In the thicket, on the hill:
But a rarer flower in a lonely bower,
  Adown in the dale below,
'Mong stranger vines, all drooping pines,
  Bereft of each kindred blow.
And a sweeter bird is often heard,
  On the long, long summer day,
Of its early home, over ocean's foam,
  A singing a plaintive lay:
Oh! wilding rare, no longer wear
  That gloom in your fragrant breast;
Oh! Birdie bright, mourn not the light,
  The light of your rifled nest.
Thus spoke to cheer her darling dear,
  A follower, true and tried,
A follower old, of the Desmond bold,
  But Desmond's sister sigh'd,
She sigh'd full sore, and o'er and o'er
  Her bosom sighed again,
Oh! I must awake, or my heart will break,
  My heart's wild wayward strain;
In sadness strung her wild harp rung,

As her fingers moved along,
Its voice and tone, tuned to her own,
And this was the maiden's song.

SONG.

I.

I do not mourn for honors bright,
For wealth or titles high;
Nor seek for tongues that used to praise
Oh! not for these I sigh,
Give them to vain ambitious heart,
They have no charms for me;
But oh! let me behold again,
My own bright gushing Lee.

II.

Tho' foemen, rule our broad domain,
And slaves defile the place,
Where Princes of our honored line,
Swayed o'er a gallant race;
The tears that dim my vision now,
No tyrant foe should see;
If but a sheeling were my home,
Beside my natal Lee.

III.

Yon bird of dusky wing, that sings
On yonder oak so proud,

And those of gay and gaudy plume,
  Now carolling aloud,
Their songs, my heart with sadness fill,
  Alas! when shall I see
The Thrush, the Linnet and the Lark,
  Sweet songsters of the Lee.

IV.

The heart upon its natal earth,
  Views this fair hill with pride;
My heart is in a distant land,
  By that bright river's side
Where daisies deck the dewy sward,
  And blooms the Hawthorn tree:
And primrose mild, and shamrock green,
  Shine on the silver Lee.

V.

Oh! bear me to my own old land,
  Oh! bear me back once more;
That I may look on Lee's bright wave,
  That kisses her fond shore;
That I may lay my weary breast,
  Where oft it wandered free;
And sleep in peace, my lullaby,
  The murmurs of the Lee.

His charger bold, all trap'd with gold,
  Was fain to bound away;
But he would that Chevalier,
  The maiden's plaintive lay.

His smile was bright, his heart was light,
  His form of comely grace;
Oh! was it shame, or a warmer flame,
  Suffus'd his noble face;
When bending low, o'er his saddle bow;
  His helmet raised on high;
Oh, Lady fair, he cried, forbear!
  Nor thus in sorrow sigh:
The way is long, my arm is strong,
  A good ship waits for me;
I'll be thy guide, what e'er betide,
  Back to thy bonnie Lee.
Her heart grew sore, her eyes ran o'er,
  Her cheeks like lily shone;
But fonder spell, full quickly fell,
  Tho' word, she answered none:
She spoke no word my bonnie Bird,
  But there is a language sweet,
The heart will teach unknown to speech,
  When bright eyes, bright eyes meet.
Full oft again did the soldier rein
  His steed by the summer bower;
Nor truer tale did e'er prevail,
  To gladden a fonder flower.
Oh! woe betide a Brother's pride,
  A Brother's heart of steel;
That heart will bleed, whose ruthless deed
  Opposed a Sister's weal.
My Birdy's gone, My Birdy's flown,
  My Birdy's won and wed,
Over ocean's foam, to her early home,
  My bonnie Birdy's fled.

Here Hannah's story stop'd a space,
Yet still she hummed, her withered face,
Clasped by her bony hands unseen,
Beneath her hood's close folded screen,
And pressed against the vesture sheen
Of that lone grave; in slower time,
And cadence sad, she wakes her rhyme.
Now six long weeks are past and gone,
Six long, long weeks are over,
Still speeds our gallant vessel on,
Still proudly speeds the Rover ;
No land to bless our vision yet,
The lurid sun in crimson set ·
And sank the sea breeze with the sun,
Whilst clouds of crimson and of gold,
In heavy masses, bright and bold,
Their firey drapery unfold,
In the far western horizon ;
The sea is smooth as molten glass,
There's not a ripple on the ocean,
Yet breathes and moves the mighty mass,
With strong upheaving troubled motion ;
Hark ! Hark, what sounds the heart appal,
Awake each breast to woe and wonder,
Is it some distant waterfall,
Commingling with the rolling thunder ?
Now rushing, gushing strong and deep,
Each moment brings its fury nearer,
This night our barque in safety keep,
Be thine the hand, Oh Lord ! to steer her.
Our good ship rocks, our good ship reels,

Our good ship on her side is lying,
Our captain's voice like thunder peals,
Our sailors brave, aloft are hieing;
Her haulyards strong, are loosely cast,
Her spars forsake their high dominions;
Her sails are flutt'ring in the blast,
Like a wounded swan's unfolded pinions;
Our ship, she lies in sore distress,
Her rigging in the ocean trailing,
God grant our mariners success;
Forbid! such toil prove unavailing.
She rights, she slowly rights once more;
No spreading sails her yards adorning,
Two narrow sheets alone she bore,
With these she scuds the tempest scorning;
She sails full swift, she sails full free;
The wind thro' her naked rigging screaming,
Like a diver, she skims the angry sea,
In her wake, the crested billows gleaming.
The wailer paused. And thus again
Resumed her melancholy strain.
The night grows dark, oh! very dark,
The stars, their midnight watch resigning
From o'er our doom'd devoted bark,
One after one withdraws its shining;
It might have been the rising moon,
It might have been a friendly bacon,
Whose ray shone forth, but ah! full soon,
To darker gloom were we forsaken.
Danger ahead! the boatswain cried!
My heart sinks at the word of sorrow,

Below my grieving bosom hied
To mourn the hopes, I might not borrow.
Oh! fondly did young Edmond fold
Against his breast, his bosom's treasure,
And sweet, of brighter morning told,
Of hope, of home, and future pleasure.
And fairer seemed his bonnie bride,
Like rose with tempest wild contending,
And thus, her Edmond's fears did chide;
Faith, hope and love, her accents blending,
He, who in hollow of his hand,
Contains the winds, the earth and ocean,
Beholds us here, if he command
The billows wild, will curb their motion,
The winds be still, the waters sleep,
Or, if His holy will ordaining,
Our graves be in the briny deep,
My soul obeys, without complaining,
His will be done, His holy will,
What e'er it be, I question never;
One wish alone, oh, Lord, fulfil,
In life, in death, unite us ever.
Loud ring the anchor's clanking chains,
Our ship is surely rent a sunder,
She plunges, shivers, groans and strains,
That shock has nearly brought us under;
Is it a mountain's crushing mass,
A mountain, from its deep foundation,
Whose ruined rocks above us pass,
And strew our decks with desolation;
The wild, wild waves now o'er her roll,

The waters wild, her bosom filling;
Oh, Lord, preserve each christian soul,
From dread despair's, unholy chilling;
Ah! now our captain comes below,
No heart, than young McGregor's braver;
He comes to tell a tale of woe,
In pity, his speech did often waver;
Our ship is tost on the Irish coast,
On the Irish coast lies she,
All our anchors cast, she is drifting fast,
And the land is on our lee;
Our hearts to save from a watery grave,
Our homes, and our hopes to gain;
Of her masts so tall, every one of them all
Lies low in the raging main.
Now, a gallant band at my command,
A fearless and faithful few,
In our staunchest boat, are now afloat,
And lie in the lee for you:
Then hasten with me, the bell tolls three,
At four, 'twill be highest tide;
God speed you to shore, ere an hour be o'er,
And God save your bonnie bride;
Oh! when on the land secure you stand,
And look on the rolling sea,
Pray Heaven, send cheer to the brave hearts here,
Who live, or who die with me;
If our minute gun, ere the morning sun,
And our signal rockets fail,
The moaning surge will have sung our dirge,
The tempest our funeral wail.

Ah ! who will bear to a maiden fair,
The fairest in all Ardee ;
Her Duncan's fate, lest she watch and wait,
Lest hoping, she wait for me.
'Twill brighten the tear, if she should hear,
'Twill soothe my affianced bride ;
On Nannie he thought, whilst bravely he fought
Dark death, in the boiling tide.
Oh ! weary fate, in bark so frail,
On sea so stormy riding ;
But hearts that ne'er were known to quail,
Stout hearts our boat are guiding.
Her prow opposes wind and tide,
A drifting, trackless way, pursuing ;
Be thou, oh Lord, our loving guide,
Preserve our helplessness from ruin,
My bosom sickens at the sight,
That dreary dismal scene to ponder ;
Here Knockamenny's fearful height,
Carrick's black ruin frowning yonder ;
Before us roll the ocean waves,
The briny ocean's endless flowing,
Strabreagy's bar behind us raves,
In furious frothy madness glowing ;
The rocket's bright unearthly glare,
The wild, wild wilderness illuming,
The tempest howling every where,
The minute gun's terrific booming :
A light upon the water gleams ;
Perhaps a meteor's fair illusion,
It sheds again its cheering beams,

Alas! alas it wakes confusion,
Our boat is shivered 'gainst a rock,
Strange voices 'mid the waves assail us,
Our dying shrieks, our prayers they mock;
Our prayers, our shrieks, our struggles fail us,
Two women frail were found alive,
One yet remains, to tell the story;
The blighted birch doth still survive,
The oaks so proud, sank in their glory;
The fishermen who gave us cheer,
This answer made our fond enquiring,
At turn of tide no lights appear,
The minute gun no signal firing;
All night they searched, 'mid wind and rain,
'Mid cold and wet, the long night over,
That fatal shore, but all in vain;
Our fond and perished to discover,
By Doah's Isle, the stream runs deep,
And swift, and strong its ebbing motion,
That current bore our brave to sleep,
With their crushed hopes to the far ocean.
The morning show'd a darksome mass,
'Mid yonder bar's, relentless breakers,
The shore, thy natal shore, alas!
Heard the harsh yell of ruthless wreckers;
But yet, among the reckless crowd,
Were some alive to pity's pleading,
Who left their spoil to swathe and shroud,
Three bodies ghastly crushed and bleeding;
One wretch behind, alone did stay,
Whilst many a weeping eye did follow,

The triple bier, they bore that day,
By yon rude Cairn down in the hollow.
Our gallant ship, her grace defil'd,
Lies in the sand, a wreck and ruin,
Whilst ocean like a froward child,
Now spurns her toy, and now is wooing,
The lowly dillisk waves its plume,
In triumph o'er her decks unsightly,
Where erst 'mid tempest's glare and gloom,
Waved England's banner proud and brightly.
'Mong vines and gilded grapes once fair,
The clustering mussel clings, deriding,
O'er chambers desolate and drear
The sea snail noiselessly is gliding;
A giant leper, barred and bann'd,
By foul deformity attended,
Disowned alike by sea and land,
Sport of the winds, her race is ended.
The fishermen from the high seas,
When by Glasshady's Isle returning,
Oft hear upon the midnight breeze
The mermaid's moan, like maiden mourning;
Wild legends say, that drear saloon,
Is where her victims toil unceasing;
With slimy sea-weed's fringed festoon,
Her damask drapery replacing,
The frailest of her fated band,
Life's waning lamp's dim ray discloses
O'er the lowly couch of Hallowed sand,
Where silent, the pulse of her heart reposes.

I.

Oh! my fair Eveleen,
  Thou we'rt good, thou we'rt fair;
The fairest maid I've ever seen,
  Might not with thee compare;
Thy heart was light, thy bosom warm,
  Dark shadows intervene,
Thy sweetness wears a softer charm,
  My fair Eveleen, my fond Eveleen:
Thy beauty wears a treble charm,
  Thy sorrows, every heart disarm,
  My fair Eveleen.

II.

Thine eyes delicious blue,
  It was mild, it was bright,
As fringes dark as ever grew,
  On lids, transparent white,
Were raised to cheer some pilgrim old,
  Or fell in modest screen;
Whilst tender tongues, thy virtues told,
  My fair Eveleen, my fond Eveleen.
Whilst truthful tongues thy virtues told,
  No tongue, thy praises might withhold,
  My fair Eveleen.

III.

Soft silvery thy speech,
  Ever mild, ever meek;
The down upon the ripen'd peach,

Not softer than thy cheek,
That mingled with the rose's hue,
The lily's tender sheen ;
Thy tear was pure as honey dew,
My fair Eveleen, my mild Eveleen.
It flowed as free as summer's dew,
To love, and gentle pity true,
My fair Eveleen.

IV.

Thy morning light shone brief,
Sad and swift fell the blow,
That filled thy heart with deepest grief,
And quenched thy smile in woe ;
My mated dove, my turtle dove,
That tore the tendrils green,
Upspringing with a mother's love,
My fair Eveleen, my sad Eveleen,
Thy orphan knew no mother's love,
Oh! bless him from thy home above,
My fair Eveleen.

Here Hannah paused, and slowly raised,
Her prostrate breast, on Edmond gazed,
Whose arms a rustic cross embrace,
The beam, his bosom's resting place.
She gazed, and thus did yet prolong,
In happier tone, her wayward song.

V.

He is manly, he is kind,
Each dimple of his face;

And winning look, restore to mind,
  A father's noble grace.
I see a mother's mildness start,
  Where blaze a father's een,
His heart is thine, his tender heart,
  My fair Eveleen, my kind Eveleen.
His youthful heart, his loving heart,
  Of all thy virtues owns a part,
  My fair Eveleen.

VI.

No passion, harsh and proud,
  Upheaves his swelling breast;
For throbbed its swift pulsations loud,
  'Gainst Hannah's beggar vest;
May Desmond's ancient glory shine,
  And gild with ray serene,
This scion of an honor'd line,
  My fair Eveleen, my blest Eveleen
May fruit and foliage intertwine,
  Oh! flourish long this bud of thine,
  My fair Eveleen.

The singer ceas'd, and crossed her breast,
The answering echoes sank to rest,
A silent prayer, she murmur'd o'er;
Then rose upon her feet once more:
Edmond she said, I'll wander slow,
And in the valley rest below.
She bound her hood around her head,
And left the dwelling of the dead;

Nor deem its denizens forgot,
By her, who leaves the lonely spot.
As slow she winds adown the hill,
Her lips in prayer are busy still ;
Thus since that hour of gloom and care,
She led the sad procession there,
From Doah's Isle ; her lov'd and lorn,
On bier, by hands of strangers borne ;
She cancelled not her debt with gold,
But prize—of price an hundred fold,
A decade on her beads she told,
And Heaven assail'd from day to day,
For all—beneath Lag's hallow'd clay.
Oh, blessed boon ! oh, guerdon bright,
Tho' hidden from our mortal sight,
Our loved and dead—our holy faith,
O'erleaps the barriers dark, of death ;
And gently binds with silken thread,
The living faithful, with their dead :
Whilst thus her way did Hannah wind,
Her young companion lagg'd behind.
His by-gone days he ponders o'er,
And scenes of childhood notes once more.
The brook is babbling in its flow,
Along his track the daisies grow :
The noisy Daws their nestlings keep,
Where yon green ivy climbs the steep.
Full oft that ladder high and rude
He climbed to reach the youthful brood.
The herd reposes in the shade—
Wild echoes now his ears invade ;

The lordly bull his trumpet sounds,
But filled with rage its notes confounds.
From knoll to knoll the rabbits leap
Around the mountain's lower keep;
In snowy clusters graze the sheep,
Whilst farther up the giant hill
The grey-beard goats climb upward still;
On naked cliff's, unmeasured height,
The Gooshawk gloats his appetite,
With bloody beak and talons fell
On rabbit, captured in the dell.
The Eagle hovers in the sky—
His nurse, his own old nurse is nigh—
His faithful guardian, blanched and grey
As Cranny's crags—unchanged as they—
And like the rude rocks of the hill,
Robed in her ancient vesture still,
Her same old beaten path pursues
Along the brook; the sea-breeze wooes,
And with his clustering, dark locks plays;
The sun pours down his noontide rays
Where e'er he treads or turns to gaze;
Unchanged each scene of by-gone days—
Himself of all he sees is changed,
Since last by Cranny's base he ranged.
His thoughts find voice, and she who smiled—
That modest, meek, endearing child—
On boy, rough, thoughtless, rude and wild,
Does she, when wandering by this burn,
E'er wish those days of bliss return;
Or blesses she a fonder guide.

He crushed the thoughts he could not bide,
Choked in his breast the struggling sighs,
And thus began to moralize:
Oh, Hannah, what a heart is thine;
How purged of pride, how pure the shrine;
To wealth and worldly honors born,
Accepts alone its frown and scorn.
In beggar's vesture meanly dressed,
What treasures hide within that breast,
Where sanctity renews her fires
O'er human passion's crushed desires,
Where love unselfish ever glows,
And pity mourns for other's woes,
And meek humility entwines
O'er brightest worth her lowly vines;
Whilst sorrows dark, of Ebon dye,
That gall, must uncomplaining lie.
Oh breast of mine, where rising proud,
Each selfish care wakes clamours loud,
Murmurs rebellious nurse no more,
But learn of her the hallowed lore,
That sacred science, whose fond light
Makes even her wintry trials bright,
And bids her gather gold and joy
From ruined hope's dark cold alloy,
Where others ashes find. But see,
Her decade told, she waits for me.
'Twould much delay our lengthened tale
To trace their journey o'er the vale,
And by Strabreagy's wave-washed strand,
Where giant pyramids of sand,

That like grim sullen misers, rear
Their burnished bald heads, high in air,
With ragged front and brow of guile,
Each mourning o'er his wasting pile.
By toilsome track when spent the day
They reached a path whose mazy way
And grassy margin, sharply turn
By Cranny's basement, where the burn,
Tired of its brawling turns—like child
To breast maternal—silent, mild
Within Strabreagy's placid breast;
And soft as childhood sinks to rest;
Whilst near the daisied track they drew,
Their former converse they renew.
I lingered in these glens a year;
Since then I wandered far from here
Alone, where milder breezes fanned
My withered cheek in Southern land,
Yet, could not win—tho' fiercer gale
Too often here my steps assail;
That fealty, my heart alone
Gives thy green glens Old Inishowen.
A stranger to our race and creed,
And rough in speech, but kind in deed,
Is Duncan Stuart of Knockglass,
Whose strength doth other men's surpass,
But waves of mercy flood his breast:
Three days have I remained his guest,
Whilst he conveyed from Doah's shore,
The tablet, Desmond's 'scutcheon bore,
And placed it on that battlement,

That o'er its broken basement leant,
So dangerous, insecure and frail,
Whilst I would climb, fell with the gale.
Brave Duncan Stuart, Edmond cried!
Excise man's dread, and smuggler's pride;
Oft have I sat beside your still,
That graced the slope on Gorey's hill;
Oft when by comrades left alone,
Your voice would try a gentler tone,
To teach me secrets of your trade,
Might yet, my better fortune aid.
Tho' but a child, I learn'd it then,
Not by their seeming judge of men,
For some there are like Duncan, wear
Rude garb o'er virtues heavenly rare.
And some, their crimson crimes to screen,
Robe heart debased, in vesture sheen.
He helped to build, his comrade cried!
Our shelter rude on Gorey's side,
And oft increased our slender store,
When famine's shadow crossed the door.
Allusion to his early need,
Made Edmond's sorrowing bosom bleed,
Oh! had'st thou in thine hour of woe,
But let the generous Desmond know,
Tho' stubborn, hasty, harsh and rude,
Whilst anger swayed his darker mood,
Let passion's whirlwind sink to rest,
And his was mild as woman's breast;
Nor foe, nor friend in need or pain,
E'er sued for aid or grace in vain:

His sister's orphan in distress,
Had own'd his care, thy-self might press
An hundred claims, could each assign
His love to shield thy life's decline.
She stopped upon her path of sand,
And pointing with her wasted hand
Where Balagh's burn no longer led
It's troubled wave o'er rocky bed
Thro' banks where brier and buckeye thorn,
Far up the dell its track adorn,
But in the lake seeks calm repose.
Behold how soft that streamlet flows—
Not more secure its waters glide,
Commingling with Strabreagy's tide,
Than my declining years would prove,
Confiding all in Desmond's love ;
The tongue his earliest welcome told,
The arms his form did first enfold,
The lips that his did foremost press,
The hand his forehead first did bless.
Had I to Desmond then appealed,
He would have hastened, all to shield.
But, oh ! my child, I dare not brook
On Desmond's saddened brow to look ;
Tho' warm his heart, the wounds were deep—
Strange councels dark he bade me keep—
Counsels unsought, of import dread,
Suspended o'er thy father's head.
The kinder cause—his hopes to aid,
The secret trust my tongue betrayed ;
My heart might woe and want sustain,

'Twould fail at Desmond's brow of pain.
She ceased and slowly led the way
That by the streamlet's margin lay ;
Nor reck'd she of those blossoms wild,
That sweetly on her pathway smiled ;
Nor of her comrade wandering near—
For pondering o'er her past career,
Her early hopes, she sees them fade ;
Her summer's rosy dreams betrayed,
The scenes of bliss, and sin, and strife,
Through all her long eventful life;
The fair, the faithless, false and true,
In memory's mirror rise to view,
'Till down her furrowed features flow
The tears of shame, remorse and woe.
Her comrade saw and rightly guessed
The dark communings of her breast,
To sunder sorrow's galling chain
His queries thus resumes again :
My father's kin with wealth abound,
A refuge sought, had there been found,
Where woe and want, by Swilly's shore
Might dog our peaceful rest no more;
She answer made, full many a day,
That dark temptation dogged my way,
When friendless, lorn and pennyless,
Sad wanderers in a wilderness,
Where famine leagued with fever, trod,
Scourging the land with scorpion rod ;
Tho' dark as hell's eternal night,
The fiend assumed a form of light,

Making our dreary path more drear,
With contrast of that prospect fair;
But Heaven be praised, the tempter fail'd,
And grace, o'er flesh and hell prevail'd.
She sign'd the cross in reverence mild,
O'er brow and breast. And, oh! my child
What tongue the dreadful tale might tell;
Had duty failed and virtue fell,
And we traversed the easy road,
That led where worldly comforts flow'd.
Thyself, a proud apostate now,
The rebel's brand upon thy brow,
Mocking thy fair baptismal vow;
And she who led thy steps astray,
And placed thee in the tempter's way,
The deepest curse, the darkest gloom,
Intensest hell, and deadliest doom
Were hers, with more than murder dyed,
Thy ransom'd soul's infanticide.
Oh! Heaven be blessed—she cried again
The tempter's toils were set in vain,
Tho' soiled by sin, and crushed in care
Old Hannah's heart may not despair;
And thou, in lieu of worldly dross,
A soldier of our creed and cross;
A christian knight, by Christ's high grace;
The foremost front, thy birth-right place,
And may the saint's protection shine
On thee, and be their triumphs thine.
Tears, Edmond's grateful breast control,
Won by that fortitude of soul,

Whilst thus he answered, could it be,
That he, you fostered, lean from thee,
Callous as yonder crag to grow,
And faithless as the wintry snow
That blots beneath the vernal ray,
The records worn in ruder day:
The memory of those vigils drear,
Those weary years of watchful care
O'er faith's fair gem in casket frail
Its ray just rising, pure and pale,
Could still command with melting flame,
Of pity, penitence or shame,
The faithless bosom's frozen tide
To flow per force, for her, my guide,
That guardian, of the child unknown,
To win, whose weal, she spurned her own ;
Oh, cruel fate, when fortune pil'd
Her favors on that rescued child,
And to his parched lips bestowed,
The honeyed cup, where plenty flowed ;
Why dash with dark and false command,
The golden goblet from the hand
Of filial love, that might assuage
The sorrows of declining age ;
Whose cup of woe so full before,
At his neglect, must needs run o'er.
Sudden, as when from sunken rock,
The helmless ship receives a shock,
Rises, high on the billow's crest,
Recoils and sinks within its breast,
So Hannah raises her clasped hands,

And motionless, a moment stands
As statute rigid—wild her stare,
As if a serpent's deadly glare,
Her vision fixed on upper air.
Mother of mercy, be my guide,
In whispers broke. Down rebel pride
She loudly cried! dark child of hell!
She failed, she faltered—Ere she fell,
Edmond, his arms around her twine,
The sapling props the blasted pine;
Then gently laid her pulseless breast
On couch of verdant moss to rest,
Quickly her scarlet hood unties,
And gazes wistful in her eyes,
Deeming her gentle spirit flown,
His cheek as pallid as her own.
Then kneeling by her prostrate form,
Her head he pillows on his arm;
Whilst fragrant lilies droop and shed
Sweet dew-drops round that lowly head,
As if fair nature's self, beguiled
By seen so strange and tender, smiled
At her fond code inverted here,
And sealed her sanction with a tear.
Whilst Edmond thus his vigils kept
O'er her, who still unconscious slept,
A soft, serene and silent spell,
On plain and lake and streamlet fell,
The timid hare approached the dell,
Close to the shadow of her foes,
Beneath the willow sought repose;

The rabbits from their burrows strayed,
And fearless on the meadow played;
The cowen shy, his visage grave
Protruded o'er the brackish wave,
A moment eyed the grassy bank,
Spurned the fresh spray with snort, and sank
To seek his native brine again,
Alarming yonder stately crane,
Whose wings their lazy breadth expand,
To bear him from the minnow strand;
No foe in ken he folds his plumes,
And now his stately step resumes;
From lonely thorn the cuckoo calls,
Distinct and loud, whilst softer falls,
Half indistinct, from yonder grove,
The thrush's vesper song of love.
Bring here, Daguerre, thy matchless art,
Ere this fair fleeting scene depart,
And fix the muse's passing dream
Eternal, with thy magic beam;
Not then would wayward muse unknown,
O'er fond creation, half her own,
From sterner scenes of life beguiled
One heart allure; the rebel child
Who spurns old age's palsied hand;
Unawed by heaven's most high command,
Whose pride, like coals of living fire,
Sears matron old and wounds his sire.
Ah! he perchance might wander here,
And pause awhile, in his career,
Retrace his steps, his heart restore

To duty, love and peace once more.
Ambition's slave might here behold,
In these grey hairs, and bosom cold,
The utmost bound, the highest span,
Of life's triumphal arch ; where man—
Led by ambition, pride and guile,
Alone, may build his babel pile
Of hopes unholy, bold and vain :
Ah ! well, if he his heart arraign,
Spurning the fabric madly plann'd,
Nor build high hopes on arch of sand.
And seraph beauty, here might own
Her reign usurp'd, her vacant throne,
The empty niche, the ruined shrine,
Where erst she smiled with grace divine,
Her lilies fair, her roses red,
Deflower'd, dishonor'd, dark and dead ;
Vase, flowers, and pedestal o'erthrown,
Their ashes here, their odors flown,
Weep, beauty weep, these are thine own ;
Nor deem the muse with cynic sneer,
Thy ashes mocks, her saddest tear,
Would fall o'er yonder loveless clay;
But it emits a purer ray
From gem transcendant, whose fond light,
Like Borealis of the night,
When beams terrestrial, all are gone,
Sheds o'er life's western horizon,
Such radiant, yet mysterious ray,
That beauty's self, might weeping say
Such night is lovelier than my day.

Oh! what were beauty's brightest flame,
Reft of that gem I need not name?
A wildfire beacon, false, impure,
Placed on life's dreary marshy moor,
The soul's decoy from chaster bliss,
The light that looms o'er crime's abyss.
Forego fond muse, thy moral strain;
Thy precepts and thy preaching vain.
Vain as thy verse, yet bid it flow,
It sooth's at least, one bosom's woe;
And cheers when adverse winds assail
His struggling bark; resume thy tale.
As flows half frozen sluggish stream,
Beneath chill winter's churlish beam,
So life's returning tide once more
Old Hannah's heart is flooding o'er,
As chill, as cheerless, and as slow;
But when her comrade marked its flow,
Such wave impetuous swept his breast
As torrent shows on mountain's crest,
When fallen crags usurp its course,
And briefly bar its swelling force;
Increased in power by being pent,
It bursts the rocky battlement.
Wild, warm and free, life's current flowed,
'Till Edmond's cheeks and bosom glowed.
On his flushed features Hannah gazed
In silence, then her eyes upraised,
And suppliant hands to heaven above,
Kind heaven, she prayed, reward this love;
This duteous child's unselfish care,

A flowery path for him prepare ;
Let plenty, peace and pleasure shed
Their heavenly radiance o'er his head;
Or, if in peril, pain or need,
Be instant succor aye his meed ;
And love, if earthly love beguile
His youthful heart, oh ! let her smile
Wake flame as pure as e'er found rest
In the dark chambers of the breast.
Lend me thine aid, we will repair
Once more to our old granite chair,
Whose primrose cushion, soft and dry,
And woodbine woven canopy,
Oft gave us rest in days gone by ;
And there relenting, I'll unfold
For Mary's sake, how pride controlled
My guilty breast, to act the part
That robbed of hope her guileless heart,
And made you, by that falsehood led,
Believe your aged guardian dead.
Now Edmond's hand, with tender care,
Helps Hannah climb the lofty chair.
It was a fair, fantastic throne,
That moss-grown Druid Alter stone,
Whose breast, tradition tells, was wore
In channels thus by human gore,
So often flowed the purple tide,
So oft the vestal victim died
In rite unholy, gloomy, dread ;
And tales are yet by rumor spread,
That pilgrims 'neath its shadow still

Oblations make, and vows fulfill;
Bidding warm bosoms bleed unseen
Beneath its canopy of green,
When in the summer's balmy air
Young love usurps the Druid's chair.
Where now such idle tales to chide,
Old age and youth sit side by side;
To both, awhile, we bid adieu,
The muse must other scenes pursue.

END OF FOURTH CANTO.

FRIAR'S CURSE—CANTO FIFTH.

The noon-day sunbeams, brightly played
With Gorey's runlet in the glade,
Yet vainly strove fair Goreymore,
Thy haunted hazel dells explore ;
When by the brook within the glen,
And scarcely seen, two silent men
Ascend the slope that climbs a space,
Halfway 'twixt Gorey's crown and base ;
One seems in prime of manhood's pride,
Huge is his frame, and firm his stride,
Whilst Atlas like, his shoulders bear
The cumb'rous copper still in air ;
And twin'd around the darksome mass,
His brawny arms seem bands of brass.
The other, young of slender form,
Bends 'neath the load of head and worm ;
Oh ! not to gain all Inishowen,
Would gauger dare, tho' armed, alone
Approach that covert in the hill,
To confiscate the mountain still,
If stood, to sentinel the pass,
Bold Duncan Stuart of Knockglass,
Who makes old Gorey's caves resound,
As falls his burden to the ground ;
But hark ! why echoes Gorey's glen

With laughter loud of joyous men?
Perhaps a foot-race has been run;
Perhaps a cock-fight's lost and won;
Perhaps dame Fulton bore a son,
Her Lord to bless, and blithmeat cheer,
He gives his auld acquaintance here;
There is no race on yonder green,
Nor cock, nor cockpit here is seen;
Dame Fulton bore no son to bless
The anxious Lord; yet, I confess,
Could you her bursting bodice view,
You'd promise Rab not one but two;
No christening here, nor wedding feast,
No holy station of the priest,
Nor churn *; before, nor since, was known
A feast like this in Inishowen.
Do thou with me prolong thy stay,
And list the muse's livelier lay.
To her is known each form and face,
And dwelling of that mountain race;
These all were smugglers in their day,
And hale and hearty still, tho' grey;
And bold and fierce in fight, but met
In peace, they, former feuds forget.
For there is Darrig, of the Croah;
Red Rory, of Slieve Bawn;
McColgan, of the Isle of Doah;
McCallion, of the Strand;
Black Phelemy, of Malin Well;
And white-haired Art-A-Friel;
And Donald Roe Mc'Con-A-Gael,

* Harvest home.

The Chief of Ballagh Neal;
McLaughlin, he of Gorey Beg;
Cresswell, of Carramore,
Whose leather side and wooden leg,
A fearless bosom bore;
And honest Mannes, of the mill,
With heart and hand so free,
He loves a joke, he loves a gill;
Big Bunnocks loveth he;
From Ballagh, Duncan Campbell came;
O'Doherty from the brae;
Auld Rabin Lindsey frae Cauld Hame,
  From Killian glen McRae;
And Billy Bogs, the hero bold,
  Now Lord of ancient Lag;
Who rode his horse up Cranny's hold,
  And leap'd the mountain crag.
And others, I could name a score;
  Brave men, whose deeds of fame,
Shine still in legendary lore,
  That I forbear to name.
Here Hugh O'Donnel bold and free,
  With open hand and smile,
Welcomes with martial courtesey
  Each 'lated guest the while,
For he would feast his friends at home,
  Proud host to gallant men,
The banquet spreads beneath the dome
  Of Heaven, in Gorey's glen;
One child, and graceful as a Fay,
  O'Donnel's household star,

Glides 'mong these reveling vet'rans gray,
  Like peace, 'mong hosts at war;
And oft her black and brilliant eye,
  When but the muse might tell,
With down cast look, and glimmer sly,
  Would wander down the dell;
But whether 'twas in bashfulness,
  Her look went down the glen,
As round her twin'd in light caress,
  The arms of gray haired men.
Or, whether Duncan's young compeer,
  Who trimmed his still below,
Had ought to do with Nannie's leer,
  I know not; this I know,
By accident their glances met
  An equal space between:
As dark clouds hide the lightning's jet,
  Did Nannie shroud her een—
The sunbeams laughing dyed her face,
  With rich and rosy stain;
And interven'd a treble space,
  E're Nannie gleek'd again—
The mountain dew flows round and round,
  Round goes the social smoke,
And care, if care they knew, is drown'd
  In sparkling bowl and joke,
Whilst tales are told of youthful strife,
  And bold adventures sung,
Till veterans on the verge of life
  Deem they again are young.
No fetters curb the free-born mind,

Nor clog the bounding heart;
Their mirth flows free as flows the wind
That mocks all powers of art;
It flows as flow their mountain streams—
A torrent loud and strong—
Till Art-A-Friel an audience claims—
Then mirth makes way for song.

SONG—"THE MILLER OF MALIN."

I.

Now all ye good people, I pray lend an ear;
I won't keep you long if you're willing to hear;
A wonder of wonders I mean to expoun':
There's a miller that's honest, resides at Mill Town;
With a word of his mouth he will banish the dumps;
Has cures for the chin cough, the measels and mumps;
The quinsy, the colic, the toothache that jumps.
All these has the miller of Malin;
Then drink to the miller of Malin.
What never was known in old Inishowen,
There's an honest good miller in Malin.

II.

The night before last, as I rode from the Fair,
With a drop in my head, on my bonnie grey mare,
Two women—my neighbors—did talk, I'll be boun';
And they talk'd of the miller that lives at Mill Town.
Says Betty to Biddy, 'twas just at New Year,
He baked me the Bunnock and bid me good cheer;

My apron—she whispered something in her ear.
    God bless the old miller of Malin;
    Then drink to the miller of Malin.
    What never was known in old Inishowen,
    There's an honest good miller in Malin.

III.

And there's Katy Collins that lives at the rock,
She told me wee Jamie was sick with the pock;
His throat it was sore, not a drop would go down
Till she went to the miller that lives at Mill Town;
He asked for three bottles, unlicens'd and pure;
She brought him the best—he drank one at the door.
The sicker the Bairnie, the harder the cure.
    So answered the miller of Malin;
    Then drink to the miller of Malin.
    What never was known in old Inishowen,
    There's an honest good miller in Malin.

IV.

Friend Katy, says he, and he pinched her right arm;
Tell no one the secret, 'twould banish the charm,
These bottles I bury, must never be foun';
Then took he, that miller of bonnie Mill Town,
The empty black bottle, and held to the spout
Where a hole in the race let the mill water out;
Here's ready relief, and a cure without doubt.
    'Twas thus spoke the miller of Malin;
    Then drink to the miller of Malin.
    What never was known in old Inishowen,
    There's an honest good miller in Malin.

V.

And Peggy Gillespie, this story does tell;
Before she got married to Dave at the well,
Imagined her Davie grew cold and unsoun';
So she went to the miller that lives at Mill Town;
Oh! miller, a maiden from sorrow to save,
From sorrow that's leading her fast to her grave,
Tell what shall I do to restore me my Dave.
Tell me, honest miller of Malin;
Then drink to to the miller of Malin.
What never was known in old Inishowen,
There's an honest good miller in Malin.

VI.

He look'd on her cheeks, they were hollow and wan,
He gazed in her eyes, and examined her han';
He gathered each shadow, and noted it down,
All this did the miller of bonnie Mill Town;
I know of a potion would Davy restore
To love, till the days of his courtship be o'er,
But win him, and wed him, a thousand times more
He'll rue. Said the miller of Malin;
Then drink to the miller of Malin.
What never was known in old Inishowen,
There's an honest good miller in Malin.

VII.

I see by the crosses impressed on your palm,
A fairy has rifled your lips of there balm,
Three kisses unblighted, thy maiden-hood crown;

Lack a-day, says the miller that lives at Mill Town;
The first is a father's, my father is dead.
A miller that's honest and owns a grey head,
And has bairns of his own, he may take it instead.
    Then kissed her; the miller of Malin;
    Then drink to the miller of Malin.
    What never was known in old Inishowen,
    There's an honest good miller in Malin.

VIII.

The next is a mother's. A mother I've none;
Nor sister, nor brother—I'm lonely and lone.
Give me, who did ne'er on the fatherless frown,
That kiss; says the miller that lives at Mill Town.
Now woe, bonnie lassie, the direst of woe,
If you upon mortal the last one bestow—
Be he lover so kind, be he friend, be he foe.
    So said the old miller of Malin;
    Then drink to the miller of Malin.
    What never was known in old Inishowen,
    There's an honest good miller in Malin.

IX.

So keep it and care it; unlucky the day
For Peggy, if willing she give it away,
'Till a bride at the altar; so fate has writ down.
And so says the miller of bonnie Mill Town.
Now Davy and Peggy long wedded they be;
She's a bird on her breast and a bairn by her knee,
And a tear will aye peep frae the tail of her ee
    When you speak of the miller of Malin;

Then drink to the miller of Malin.
What never was known in old Inishowen,
There's an honest good miller in Malin,

X.

If any be bairnless who hearken my tale,
Send your wife to the mill with a melder* of meal;
Let her measure the toll in the skirt of her gown,
And give to the miller that lives at Mill Town.
He'll bake her a Bunnock a housewife may eat;
If Duncan's not hen-pecked—I'll wager my pate—
In less than a year, or the miller's a *cheat*,
Old Mannes, the miller of Malin.
So here's to the miller of Malin;
The witty old miller of Malin.
What never was known in old Inishowen,
There's an honest good miller in Malin.

Old Gorey's deepest caverns rung
With echoes loud and long,
When Art gave o'er; for every tongue
Proclaimed his "health and song;"
And hands grasped hands in heart's delight,
That oft, in days of yore,
When blood was up in factious fight,
Reeked with each other's gore.
But feud of clan, of kin, of creed,
Lies buried here to-day,
And friendly speech and peaceful deed,
Inspire each clansman grey;

* A grist.

Full warm their heart's best feelings flow,
  And mirth resounds amain,
Till Art bids all, their mirth forego,
  And list a maiden's strain.
Close clinging to her father's chair,
  And gleeking down the glen ;
O'Donnel's youthful daughter there
  Beguiles these aged men.

SONG.

I.

The thrush sat silent on the bough,
  That sweetly sang the live-long day ;
The flocks lay sleeping on the knowe,
  Whilst day light softly stole away.
My heart was sad, I may not say
  What sorrow ruled my bosom then ;
When 'neath the twilight's gentle ray,
  I wandered up to Killian glen.

II.

I marked the daisy on the green,
  I mark'd the primrose in the dell ;
The cowslips 'neath the hazel screen,
  The hawthorn's bloom, and sweet blue-bell,
Soft was the charm that soothing fell,
  And ruled my pensive bosom then ;
But flower more bright, and fonder spell,
  My heart allur'd to Killian glen.

III.

Her form is like an angel, fair;
  Her cheeks are blooming as the rose;
Around her snow-white neck, her hair
  In silken ringlets sportive flows:
Her eye beam curtain'd in repose,
  Rewards my warm and wilder'd ken;
But soon those uprais'd lids disclose
  A dazzling ray in Killian glen.

IV.

Oh! were I king on England's throne,
  Or monarch grand of mighty Spain;
Or did I all the riches own,
  The famed Peruvian mines contain;
I'd barter all, ten times again,
  And deem my treasure priceless then;
To win my bonnie blue eyed Jane,
  The lovely flower of Killian glen.

'Tis said that music's magic spell,
Can smooth the brow of care;
Suspend, uplifted weapon fell,
Of savage, in the air.
Allure the serpent from the fen,
And blunt his barbed sting;
Delay the tiger in his den,
Yea, charm the forest king:
But music, all thy power is vain,
Vain is thy Heaven born art,

To soothe the rankling love lorn pain
In slighted rival's heart.
Now tender was the maiden's lay
As maiden's lay might be ;
And aged men were there to say,
'Twas sweetest melody ;
Still passion's fierce, and thoughts unblest,
And haughty high disdain,
Broke Duncan Stuart's bosom's rest
Whilst Nannie sung her strain.
For rumour did a tale declare,
And spread it far and wide,
That he, to Killian's Jeannie fair,
Made suit last Lammas tide ;
But sued in vain, and since that hour,
Within his breast, a flame,
All tender throbs consumes, whose power,
Not music's charms may tame.
At yonder festive board, no right
Of guest, may Duncan show ;
Yet of the revelers in sight,
Much he desired to know :
But not till Nannie's tender song
Had prob'd his wounds anew,
Gained he the resolution strong
To join the gallant crew.
Brave Duncan Stuart welcome here,
The Host rejoicing said ;
Rose at that name a mighty cheer,
And rose each hoary head.
Fill up, Auld Rabin Lindsey cried,

Brave Duncan, fill your glass;
The toast is Andy Campbell's bride,
Once Killian's lovely lass.
As looks the eagle when the crow
Presumptuous mars his way,
As warrior's eyes, unworthy foe,
With deepest scorn survey,
So Duncan's eyes Auld Rabin view,
And all who stand around;
Then in a bowl of mountain dew,
His rising choler drown'd.
I wud na' gie' my bonny ewe,
He muttered forth in scorn,
That's milking in the fauld below,
For a' the women born;
Put L to ass, and there's a Lass,
Alas, there's something wrong.
Come fill once more each man his glass,
In honor of my song;
The revelers 'round the table drew,
And pour'd the potent flood,
Duncan his brawny arms out threw
Above, like beams of wood;
With one he pointed down the glen,
Where steams his mountain still;
Loud o'er the roar of mirthful men,
His song alarms the hill.

SONG—"THE BONNIE BLACK EWE."

1.

The lover may liken his simpering maid
To a bright summer primrose in dew-drops array'd,
And gossips cry, joy and good fortune betide,
On the morn of their marriage, both bridegroom and
bride.
The bridal wreath's, bonnie and fragrant, I own,
But thorns will be found when the blossoms are flown,
For beauty is fleeting, and love will grow cold,
Like the ray of the sun when the summer is old ;
Then husband who's henpeck'd, and darna' complain,
Would you ken what would lighten your pettycoat
pain?
Lest Betty might hear it, I'll whisper it low:
Drink the milk that I draw from my bonnie black ewe.
Singing fol de rol, lol de rol, ee.

II.

The priest of the parish will tell you at mass,
To banish my ewe's milk and wed you a lass ;
The Padre is wise, and by the same rule,
If he practised his preaching, I'd ca him a fool;
Our minister tells us at prayer-meeting time,
To drink to excess is a damnable crime;
If to lie on ones back, one must hold by the ground,
The same is a drunkard—that doctrine is sound;
And the parson who prays and oppresses by turns,
Now drives for his tithes, now our ignorance mourns,

Still nurses the gout in his loyal big toe,
With the milk that I draw from my bonnie black ewe,
Singing fol de rol, lol de rol, ee.

III.

My ewe is the pride of the mountain and dale,
She comes in her season and lambs without fail;
I give her good hire, both of barley and corn,
And free flows the milk, like a stream thro' her horn;
When the mists on the brae bid the wolves leave their den,
I watch the red prowlers and keep them in ken;
In the mirk o' the night I am ay by her side;
I love her more dear than the bridegroom his bride,
For jarring and jealousy often prevail,
If Rab be a churl, or Betty be frail;
And Betty and Rabin, as all of you know,
Love the milk that I draw from my bonnie black ewe,
Singing, fol de rol, lol de rol, ee.

The banquets bursting swelling flame,
The muse must here forego;
Imperfect art, and spirit tame,
And language dull and slow,
Image the rushing roaring streams,
That round its circle run;
As faint as Cynthia's eclips'd beams,
Portray the glorious sun.
Yet long they held rude revelry
On Gorey's grassy side;
And bountiful the feast, and high,

Now view its ebbing tide ;
The smoking trenchers, all are gone,
Gone all the varied cheer ;
The goblet, flask and bowl alone,
In files confused, appear :
Like foremost rank of serried host,
At close of battle's day ;
They faithful keep their fated post,
Tho' broke their fair array.
Ye strangers to our glens, who deem
From my unpolished song;
That actions rude, alone be seem,
These men of impulse strong ;
Know ye, that 'neath the roughest rind,
Is core the sweetest found.
That gems, whose mildest sparkles blind
Hide in ungainly ground.
That craggy hill and mountain stern,
And moorland bleak and drear,
Have nooks where bloom the fragrant fern,
Mild heath and primrose fair,
Behold ! e'vn now those veterans rude,
Of varying creed and race,
Their heads down bowed, their hearts subdued ;
Of boisterous mirth no trace,
For Mary's harp in tones of woe,
Thrills to the magic stroke ;
And calm as yonder lake below,
The sounds that late awoke ;
It was as sweet and sad an air,
As harper ever played ;

Lament, and anguish, yea despair,
Each spell-bound ear invade.
O'Donnel asks, to air so wild,
Are there no words belong?
Ah! they are sad replied his child,
A Royal captive's song,
Our festal day, 'twould mar and warp,
Such anguish there is blent;
Oh! sing they cry. She woke the harp
And sang the sad lament.

LAMENT OF THE CAPTIVE QUEEN.

I.

Ah! me, a weary captive, what avails,
That my salt tears, like ocean's endless flow,
In tide perpetual rise: My sighs in gales
Swell to high Heaven, freighted with grievous woe;
The morning sun from nature's virgin face,
Steals the fond tear drops with his warm caress,
Alas, no radiant beams my tears erase,
Ah! me, sad hapless Queen in bitterness,
All desolate and lone, I sorrow to excess.

II.

Oh! cruel tyrant, from my regal brow,
With ruthless hand, you tore my diadem,
And since your hour of triumph, until now,
My anguish mock, my plaintive cry contemn;
You bid me banish from my anguish'd mind

My early love, still partner of my woe,
And turn to thee. Does the poor stricken hind
Turn to the hound, the turtle to the crow,
I to thy foul embrace? No, violator, no.

III.

'Reft of my birthright dower, my fair domain
To foemen parcell'd, who in blood delight;
My castles level'd, their defenders slain,
My children murdered in their mother's sight;
Rich shrines despoiled, fair temples overturn'd,
Or prostituted to some purpose vile;
Oh! sainted martyrs, you who long sojourned
With me in bondage drear; your hallow'd pile
Behold! unholy rites the sacred fanes defile.

IV.

Ah! wretched me, by royal birth a queen,
My former glory mocks my present care.
What am I now? To think what I have been—
My hands I wring, my heart sinks in despair:
Commerce inviting to each busy mart,
And fleets unnumber'd hast'ning to the call;
Religion, science, and her sister art,
Adorning, guiding, sanctifying all;
Did glory like to mine e'er set 'neath darker pall?

V.

The rebel ocean, ceaseless in its roar,
Harsh, hoarse and angry, leaguing with my foe,
My fair Armadas, from a friendly shore,

Buried in utter ruin; woe on woe.
The chains I wear are eating out my life,
My heart is sick and sad, my soul no rest
Thro' the long dreary day of hopeless strife,
And drearier night of slavery unblest,
Doth harbor as of old; grief ever is her guest.

VI.

Ye heavens that o'er me frown, what have I done
That from my vision you your radiance veil?
My womb prolife bore no recreant son,
No daughter nurtured I whose virtues fail.
Oh! look with pity on a mother's pains,
Thou to whose fiat still I bend the knee;
Oh keep me faithful, tho' my life blood drains,
My martyr'd children's agony to see,
Ev'n tho' the crown be mine thou gavest Machabee.

Oh, wayward, wild, presumptuous muse,
Too weak thy artless hand
To image music's mighty spell
On that stern, silent band.
Come thou where flowers the sweetest wave,
Beneath the foliage bright;
Come where the thrush and linnet sing,
From morn 'till dewy night;
Come where on bowers more fresh and fair,
Has summer's sun ne'er shone,
Or lovers stole, love's tales to tell,
And love's fond empire own;
Come thou where nature's beauties reign,

These rightfully belong
To nature's own untutor'd child ;
Awake thy softer song.
Whilst yet, the maiden's minstrel power,
The banquet ruled ; to Gorey's bower
Glentogher's maid, her footsteps turned,
And for her absent lover mourned.
Tho' joy resounds on hill and vale,
And fragrant odors freight the gale ;
The tears well up in Ellen's eyes,
And in her bosom sobs arise,
Till breaking forth in plaintive song,
She owns the cares her bosom throng.

SONG.

I.

The day is now declining love,
  The hour of hope is gone ;
My soul in grief repining love,
  I wander here alone.
Bright flowers unfold their freshest bloom,
  The breeze is freighted with perfume,
Sweet voices cheer the dell and grove,
  But I still mourn my absent love.

II.

I came at early morning love,
  I sought the trysting tree ;
Again at eve's returning love,

I watch and wait for thee.
I hear the thrush's voice elate,
I see his love enraptured mate ;
Her quivering wings, her transport prove,
Yet, I still mourn my absent love.

III.

These flowers I cull, are grieving love,
Their tears, my breast bedew,
They feel its wild upheaving love,
They know it throbs for you.
Oh ! come and bid my sorrows flee,
The birds are singing merrilie,
They sing to mock yon lonely dove,
That mourns like me, its absent love.

A coming footfall wand'ring near,
The singer paused, in hope and fear,
Perhaps 'tis he, her longing breast
In silent thought, the hope confessed.
An instant more, and from the glade
Our youthful hero forth essayed.
Ah, fair enchantress, weaving spells
For wanderers in these fairy dells ?
He press'd her hand, bewitching Fay,
How many hearts have bled to-day?
She answered, blushing, all my art
Has fail'd to reach one stubborn heart ;
Wild from the mark flew ev'ry shaft ;
A very bungler in the craft,
To cupid's arts I'll bid farewell,

And school my heart in peace to dwell;
To thee, love's bold, defiant foe,
I here resign this useless bow.
Dissembler fair, the youth replies,
What of the archery of thine eyes?
Though thou resign the bowman's art,
These hold no truce with mortal heart.
Ellen, too, conscious of their sway,
All blushes, turn'd her gaze away;
Confused, abashed, the curtain drew,
And veil'd the radiant orbs from view.
Then loud arose the wassail cry,
Laughter and song and revelry:
What merry band holds revel near?
What! Ellen cries, didst thou not hear
Of gath'ring of the mountain men
At Hugh O'Donnell's, in the glen?
Old Art, the sage of Carramore,
Deep read in our prophetic lore;
Ogham and script he quotes at will,
From Druid priest to Columb Kille;
Before these patriarchs, grave and bold,
The Friar's mystic curse unroll'd;
Show'd clear as sun illumes the sky,
Fulfillment of the prophesy.
This day, the twenty-fourth of June,
The clansmen's long neglected boon—
When heirless chiefs their scepters yield,
Or rival leaders take the field;
Restor'd their chieftian's former sway.
They hold high festival to-day·

And never yet this mountain band
Obeyed more gallant chief's command.
Now, rumor says, since Christmas tide,
That chief is oft by Mary's side;
And well I note her radiant eye
More brightly beams whilst he is nigh,
And well believe, her breast returns
The tender flame his bosom burns;
Now hark! the minstrel maiden's strain:
She wakes the song of love again.
Deep, Ellen prob'd the stranger's breast,
That long had harbored love's unrest;
And well she played her subtle part,
To reach the secret of his heart;
For, as she closed her specious tale
His youthful brow, shone sad and pale,
The ruined hopes of long, long years,
O'erflowed his soul, where true love sears,
And riots o'er the ruined fane;
Yet not a word betrayed his pain,
Laggart she cries! I mourn thy fate,
He woo's to loose, who woo's too late,
Let hope within thy breast expire;
The mountain chief—is Mary's sire.
He stood unmoved, the sudden shock
Of shattered hopes, like rifted rock;
But tears came stealing to his eyes,
When Ellen spoke her fond surprise.
Ah! cruel maid, he now replied,
I own the flame I cannot hide,
Yet far beyond thine aim, thy dart

Fell on my wounded grieving heart.
Yon lonely tottering roofless shed,
Has canopied, my infant head;
This lovely hill in years gone by,
Has echoed my exultant cry,
Oft in the long bright balmy hours,
Have I traversed its verdant bowers,
Oft culled its flowers in summer's pride,
And sported oft in yonder tide.
Tho' doomed in distant lands to roam
My heart clung to its early home,
Whilst absence, gilding each rude spot,
The dark ravine, the fairy grot,
Bade fancy with enchanting power,
Weave charms around its humblest flower;
To crown each dream my fancy wove,
Of hill and dale, of lake and grove;
One gentle maid, with charms divine,
Still seem'd to link her fate with mine,
Love woo's me to her calm retreat,
To lay my sorrows at her feet.
Surprise and doubt woke Ellen's sigh,
As cold she made the youth reply;
Why? when beneath our humble roof,
You, from your treasure kept aloof:
Then might you well your suit commend,
Her father there—he was your friend;
What urgent haste your footsteps woo'd?
Or was our mountain home so rude,
Nor friend—nor love—could there delay,
Your restless wand'rings but a day?

And why so long—if love divine,
Thy soul inspire, neglect the shrine?
Oh, gay deceiver! maid will fail,
In duty, who would trust thy tale.
Ah! there was other council given,
Edmond replied, that day kind Heaven
Restored the father to his child,
When I misled—His truth defiled—
I urged him name the wand'ring guest,
Unknown—your generous kindness blest,
And let me, 'neath his friendly eye,
The conquest of her bosom try;
But this his guardian mind denied,
And wounded love, and youthful pride.
Thus he decreed—A father's care,
And right paternal, first would share
The maiden secrets of her breast,
Lest I intrude on chosen guest,
And by the charms of childhood's claim,
Or wealth, that gilds my youthful fame,
Might warp the yielding heart to guile,
And true love's temple fair defile.
If Mary's breast to love betray'd,
By her own choice, was captive made,
So would her father me advise,
And I my claims must sacrifice.
By honor bound, I pledged my hand,
To flee at once my native land,
And in my home of wealth and pride,
Beyond the sea, my passion chide;
If still her maiden breast were free,

As on the day she wept with me,
When my old nurse with bleeding heart,
Tore our enfolding arms apart,
Then I were free—Oh! blissful boon,
This four and twentieth day of June,
In ancient gorey's fairy glen
My suit to press, tho' bann'd till then;
And he, the secret unbetray'd
Of my nativity, would aid
My tender claims, when home's sweet rest
Restor'd to bliss his weary breast,
Whilst tales of other lands beguiled,
His treasures twain, and partner mild,
Tales of fierce hosts in deadly strife,
Of captive hours and peril'd life;
But brighter still, of gen'rous deed
By foeman; in his direst need.
Ah, who but those who loved as well
As I, can of my anguish tell?
When by my compact bound and bann'd,
I mutely kissed her virgin hand;
And hurrying down Glentogher's side,
Abandon'd bliss at Christmas tide.
Now, gentle Ellen, find some way
Thy absent cousin to waylay,
And to my venture lend thine aid.
Forgive, forgive me, Ellen said,
In my light jest I never dream'd
That thou wert other than you seem'd;
A waif, by winds adverse delay'd,
A star that from its orbit stray'd.

Where yonder runlet glides unseen,
Beneath the poplar's silver screen,
Close by the beach, a charming bower—
I'll wile her there at vesper hour.
But see, she comes, our ambush plann'd;
I'll meet you by the lakelet's strand.
Edmond descended Gorey's bowers,
But Ellen stoop'd to gather flowers,
Twining a wreath of richest bloom,
And working charms for Mary's doom.
'Twas thus the fair magician's art
Wove tender toils to snare the heart.

SONG.

I.

He said he would make me a lady of state,
With a palfrey to ride and a page to attend;
I would live in a castle all lordly and great,
With a moat to surround it and keep to defend.
He told he'd deck me in tissue of gold,
And promised to love me and make me his bride;
But I thought of the days of my childhood—And cold
O'er my heart came a chill—Oh! I deem'd I'd have died.

II.

The cottage of stone that was built in the Glen,
And the playmate that gamboll'd with me on the green;

Tho' humble they were—When I thought of them then,
He could not have won me to make me a Queen ;
The walls are in ruin and naked the roof,
And the playmate that loved me is far far away ;
Oh ! I'm weaving a web that has love for its woof,
And I'll wait for my true love a year and a day.

The minstrel maid to whom was known,
Each wild sweet air of Inishowen,
And every ballad love inspired,
And legend clansmen's bosom fired,
Stopped on the daisied path to hear
That ditty, stranger to her ear ;
Stopped in the shade, where roofless, lone,
Stood ivy-mantled cot of stone,
And whilst the fair entangler sung,
Her cousin's heart's-chords thrill'd and rung,
And childhood's hours again intrude,
'Till tears her thoughtful eyes bedewed.
When closed the syren's sweet refrain,
She bade her sing it o'er again,
That in her memory she might store,
Those sad, sweet words, unheard before.
'Tis, Ellen cried, a gipsy lay,
I heard it sung one summer's day ;
The words are old, the air is new,
Or else the gipsy spoke untrue.
Then sweet the echoes make reply,
To song that moistens Mary's eye,
And ere the answering echoes died,
Fled Ellen, down the glen's green side.

Behind her, Mary still delayed,
Then from the ivy tore a braid;
Immortal leaf, truth's emblem rare,
She cried, and twined it with her hair;
I love thee more than brightest flower,
Then sought at once the sea-side bower;
And when she reached Strabreagy's shore,
She hears the syren's voice once more;
It issues from the leafy glen,
But from what nook, beyond her ken.
Her song resounding thro' the dell,
Had it on stranger's hearing fell,
Doubt not, but he had told that day,
How he had heard the mountain fay;
E'en Mary's heart throbbed with surprise,
Tho' conscious of the fair disguise.

SONG.

I.

Oh! ye spirits who dwell in forest and fell,
  And call this fair mountain your own,
Elf goblin, and sprite, and fairy so bright,
  Retire to your castles of stone.
Haste away, haste away, for a goddess to-day,
  Descending from regions above,
Now reigns in these bowers 'mong foliage and flowers,
  Restoring the empire of love.

II.

And pure as the flow of the waters below,

A damsel all lovely appears;
Oh, goddess! decree that she bow unto thee,
And atone her defection in tears.
Thou handmaid of Jove send the archer of love,
Let him muffle his shafts from her eyes,
Tho' adamant vest encircles her breast,
At the sight of love's missiles she flies,

III.

Young hearts have drank pain, bright lips spoke in vain,
And Cupid exhausted his quiver;
In her prowess and pride all his parlies denied,
And a truce she has granted him—never.
Let a deep ambuscade for her bosom be laid,
And love in strange mantle enclose him;
Should he conquer to-night, that rebel so dight,
No mortal dare henceforth oppose him.

She hushed her warbling to divide
The leafy boughs her covert hide,
Shook from the canopy the dew
That gathered there; then passing thro',
Bright as a seraph from above,
And fragrant as the breath of love,
Before her cousin took her stand,
And raised aloft a hazel wand,
With flowers entwined; thus fancy wild
The syren's tuneful tongue beguil'd:
Fair maiden, I come from the region of bliss,
Where love holds his court and disposes of hearts;

I've charms in my truncheon : if ought be amiss,
  I've cures for the heart's ache and balsam for smarts;
On searching the records, 'tis found, long ago
  A germ of affection had entered thy breast,
Thou'st tenderly nursed it unhealthy and slow ;
  It only encumbers the soil it possessed ;
It needs the fond glow, loving looks can inspire,
  When eyes speak the language the lips won't confess,
It lacks the wild passion, that love glowing fire,
  When bright lips meet bright lips in honeyed impress.
So the court in its wisdom unerring, dereed,
  No longer thou'lt cherish the cold pineing sprout;
And calls it a barren and profitless weed,
  That you, from your bosom must quickly root out:
Besides, there's an item on debtor account;
  A bond for love's tribute, and long over due,
The court now proposes to square the amount,
  By blotting old scores, and begining anew :
But still if some tendril thy heart interlace,
  Or, conscience thy former short comings upbraid ;
Behold how the charms in my truncheon efface,
  What ever the bright coming future would shade.

The flow'ry wand the speaker prest,
Instanter 'gainst her cousin's breast;
Before the blushing maid could speak,
'Tis done, she cried ! 'tis thus we break
The feeble bands, that folly wove,
To bind the youthful heart from love ;
Then loud she laughed, for wildly well
She wove round Mary's path her spell,

Each word she spoke, distinctly fell
Where Edmond stood, short space apart,
And wond'ring gazed with throbbing heart;
Whilst Mary's face with very shame
That he should hear, was crimson flame;
Then with light step, and grace all glowing,
Her long dark tresses loosely flowing;
Fair Ellen sought the lakelet's strand,
Stuck her light scepter in the sand,
And crowned it with a chaplet gay;
Then more like fabled sprite or fay,
Than mortal child, forsook the shore,
Sought the green shades of Goreymore;
And there unseen by searching eye,
Climb'd the rude pathway steep and high,
Filling the air with melody.

SONG.

I.

Mortal! if with heart of guile,
  Deep with falsehood laden;
Thou wouldst dare with lying smile,
  Woo yon lovely maiden;
Touch not thou the wreath of love,
  Fairy fingers bound it;
Lest thy reckless bosom prove,
  Spirits watch around it.

II.

Mortal! if in distant land,
  One fond heart be mourning,

Watching for thy faithless hand,
  Waiting thy returning;
Touch not thou the magic coil,
  Fairy fingers bound it,
And thy perjured heart to foil,
  Spirits watch around it.

III.

But if truth and love sincere,
  Thy fond bosom swaying,
Bid thee to the maid repair,
  Why, oh! why, delaying;
Take, oh! take, the sacred crown,
  Fairy fingers bound it,
Heaven's bright bow is bending down,
  Spirits watch around it.

IV.

Let it grace her brow of pride,
  Spells no sprite discloses,
In the magic circle hide,
  Lurk beneath the roses;
Thine the flow'ry talisman,
  Fairy fingers bound it,
Dread no danger, fear no ban,
  Spirits watch around it.
She ceased her song, yet higher still,
'Mid foliage bright climbed the steep hill,
Culling the flowers now wet with dew,
That all along her pathway grew,
Till far above the hazel screen,

Her light steps trod the turf so green ;
Where soft the sunbeams sweetly smil'd
Bright welcome to fond nature's child,
And scene more fair the wond'ring maid
Deem'd mortal eye had ne'er survey'd.
Far down below, and lull'd to sleep,
Lay fair Strabreagy, calm and deep,
Where nature in her summer dress
Gazes on her own loveliness.
Lit by the setting sun's fair beams,
The lake a polished mirror seems ;
And hill and dale and cottage lone,
And hamlet fair, as truly shone
Within its crystal bosom bright
As in the sunbeam's living light,
Where great Slieve Snaght so queenly rears
Her crest high o'er her proud compeers.
Beyond Strabreagy's sheltered bay,
To warn the mariner away,
Old Knockameny's ramparts rear
Their frowning battlements in air,
Whilst hoary ocean's surging swell
'Gainst beach and ben and barrier, fell
With fearful force and thundering sound,
Shaking the cliffs for miles around,
With streamers gay and crowded sail,
One lonely bark wooes the light gale ;
Naught else, far as the wand'ring eye
Might westward range, but sea and sky.
This wond'rous scene, so fair and rude,
In rapture wild the maiden view'd—

22

Lake, hill and sky, and sea and plain,
She scann'd them o'er and o'er again
In silent wonder. Oh! I stand
In very deed on fairy land,
She cried, at last, and Gorey bright,
I'll be thy fairy Queen this night.

SONG.

I.

Since Oughie no longer your fealty claims,
Ye spirits so gentle, make haste to fulfill
The behests of your Queen; on the sun's slanting beams
Ride around, ride around, all this bonnie bright hill,
And pause, as you pass on your chariot of fire,
To peep in each dingle, each dell and ravine,
And gift with some charm that mortals inspire,
The posies, whose perfume now blesses your Queen.

II.

'Tis done, mighty Empress, my subjects reply,
Blest cheerfulness, beams in the primrose's bloom;
Chaste prudence illumines the daisy's mild eye,
The blue-bell of meekness exhales the perfume.
The butter cup purity's jewel inurns,
Rememb'rance the violet treasures unseen;
The lily with odors of sanctity burns,
We've done all thy bidding, what further, great Queen?

III.

And the rose bud forgotten, the brightest and best,
'Tis sacred to love, cries each hovering elf:

Now fold your bright pinions my faries and rest,
  I prize it so dearly, I'll bless it myself.
Here's faithful affection, confiding and true,
  And gentle forgiveness, so holy and sheen;
And hope ever pointing to happiness new,
  These blessings receive from your fond fairy Queen.

IV.

Oh! happy the lover who wanders to-night
  And gathers the blossoms, so gifted and rare;
And happy the bosom, receives with delight
  The chaplet love places on temples more fair.
Behold! the blest emblem, I've broken the thorn,
  United the rose bud and ivy so green;
At the close of life's day, love as fresh as the morn,
  I promise—for I am love's own fairy Queen.

V.

Then gather bright posies, ye lovers so true,
  The primrose and daisy and lily so fair:
The butter-cup bright, and the violet blue,
  Whose fragance like incense ascends on the air.
The rose with its blush, and the bonny blue-bell,
  That sheds like to virtue, its odors unseen;
Oh! weave me a wreath, and I'll weave you a spell,
  All potent in love; I'm the great fairy Queen.

The singer stooped to cull a flower,
That bloomed within the rustic bower;
And whilst the bud she strove to bind
Her soaring fancy's wing confined.

Not her's the voice that wakes again,
The echoes wild—Another strain,
As fond, yet more impassioned still,
Comes gently down the enchanted hill.

SONG.

I.

Great Queen of these bowers, I've culled the bright flowers,
And a wreath for my true love I'm weaving;
But sadness and care to my bosom repair,
For my long absent loved one I'm grieving;
Ah! tell, gentle fay, has she wander'd this way;
Her tears I can trace on these roses;
All fragrant and warm, her breath comes to charm;
The breeze, her soft sighing discloses.

II.

My soul's guiding star, long hidden afar,
My pathway is darksome and dreary;
Long watching in vain, its returning again,
I wander, dejected and weary;
My flocks insecure, roam the Cloghan's wild moor,
Their shepherd distressed and down-hearted,
Abandons his fold, to seek treasure untold;
For the night it is long since we parted.

III.

Oh! say, gentle Queen, if a maid thou hast seen,
Whose brow than the snow-ball is brighter;

Her cheek's blooming flush, mocks the wild rose's blush,
  Her footsteps, a fairy's not lighter ;
Her eye's mildest spark, 'neath their fringes so dark,
  A cold icy breast would set burning,
With love's fond desire, my bosom on fire,
  Its long absent love-light is mourning.

As Novice in unholy art,
From the bright world retired apart,
His Cabalistic secrets tries,
And bids some pleasing shade arise,
With horror, views a monster fell
Approach, he knows no lore to quell.
So Ellen, when the tender lay,
First came adown the mountain way,
Deemed goblin surely mocked her song,
And grief and awe her bosom throng ;
In haste her eager eyes survey'd,
The ivied rock in upland glade,
Where Oughie in the mountain hold
Held his high kingly court of old.
Now down the leafy mountain's dell,
To sue for aid, her glances fell,
But Gorey's bold projecting side,
The wand'ring ray cast in the tide.
Then gath'ring courage from despair,
She backward flung her flowing hair,
Against a mountain poplar leaning,
Far up the hill her vision straining ;
Her white hands clasp'd, seem'd to await,
All motionless, impending fate.

But soon the lover's plaintive lay
Lit in her heart a hopeful ray,
Chasing her gloomy fears away ;
On her soft cheek the lily fair
No longer droops all pallid there,
Bright rosy tints her features grace,
And smiles beam o'er her radiant face.
But when, with mournful cadence, stole
The closing stanza on her soul,
Her fluttering bosom's snowy swell,
Like ocean billows, rose and fell ;
So wild, so warm, love's promptings came,
Her lips, tho' softly, breath'd his name.
Oh ! magic word ! oh ! welcome sound !
Her Cahir hears ; with manly bound
O'erleaps the rocky barrier there,
And kneels before the maiden fair.
Her timid hand, with down-cast eyes,
She gives, and bids her love arise ;
And words of welcome, warm, sincere,
She murmurs to his raptur'd ear.
Joy of my life, began the swain,
Oh ! hour of bliss, restores again
To my lone path my angel bright,
Whose absent smile leaves dreary night.
Oh, Ellen ! if thy long delay
From our wild mountain land away,
Doomed me to many an hour of pain
And lonely toil, again, again,
Ten thousand times thy welcome dear,
Repays the breast, but thou can'st cheer ;

My treasure fond, my bosom's gem,
Receive the gifted diadem,
And all a heart so long thine own,
Has left to give, deep faith alone;
Oh! ne'er before a wreath so rare,
Pressed maiden's brow—and brow more fair
Ne'er blushed beneath the fragrant blows,
That love on loving maids bestows;
Her soft cheek rivals now the rose,
Whilst those fair drooping lids disguise,
The tears up-welling in her eyes.
But oh! that tender look expressed
Far more than words—to Cahir's breast;
Her fairy hand he fondly pressed
In both his own, with hope and fear,
Kissed from her cheek the truant tear,
That love awoke—Then murmured low,
The tender tale none else may know.
But there are those can guess;
And Ellen's answer, when it came,
O'erspread her face with warmer flame,
And did her shepherd bless:
"Thine own, dear Cahir, ever thine."
Oh! long may mutual love entwine
Its silver cord like this,
Around their hearts, when worldly cares,
Life's stern turmoil, the tempter's snares,
Assail connubial bliss.
May Heaven sustain in danger's day,
With faith and hope, their future way,
And Ellen's emblem rare,

The thornless rose, the ivy green,
Love, bright, unfailing, warm, serene,
Be thine, fond, happy pair.
Thus speaks the muse her fond farewell,
Descending Gorey's fairy dell,
Where silent, sweet Strabreagy flows,
Whose banks a kindred scene disclose.
Fair Goreymore how sweetly rang,
Thy bosom wild, whilst Ellen sang;
All placid now thine echoes rest,
Ah! how unlike that youthful breast,
Where hope and fear alternate rise,
As he, love's hap and hazard tries.
To the soft shades of Goreymore,
The bright, enchanted wreath he bore,
Where Mary, blushing, gave her hand,
And welcomed him to fairy land.
Yet sure, she cried, since thou has't seen
And heard the witching Fairy Queen,
Harsh on the ear, and cold and rude,
Must grosser sights and sounds intrude;
Yet, well believe all spells apart,
The voice is echo to the heart.
Was ever mortal blest as I?
The youthful stranger made reply;
Was ever Fay so bright before,
Or land enchanting as this shore,
Or hour, by oracle foretold,
By more propitious signs controll'd?
See, I have brav'd the dragon's glare,
And won the gifted wreath so rare,

Where spells, in blow and leaf are wove,
And guardian spirits ward in love,
Lest guile the sacred circle press,
Or aught but loveliest loveliness,
And pure as bright, the crown receive,
That fairy fingers deign'd to weave.
He placed the wreath with tender care
On Mary's blushing brow—sweet, fair,
My ordeal past, I now await
Within the magic hall of fate,
Where she, before whose throne I stand,
My weal or woe holds in her hand.
He gain'd her hand his suit to press,
But Mary's watchful tenderness,
Mourning the flame unconscious fann'd
By her fond charms, withdrew her hand.
Nay, rather flee this fairy dell,
And rend the frail, illusive spell,
The wild enchantress weaves around
Intruders on forbidden ground,
She said, and backward fled the shade,
With wistful look the hill survey'd.
Now, potent Queen, forbear to blame
If I invoke thy awful name;
A youth to free, in fatal hour,
Attracted to thy sacred bower.
Now ruled by thy bewitching power.
Ellen! the blushing maiden cried,
Ellen! the caverned hill replied,
And mountain sprites unseen, proclaim,
From keep to keep the tuneful name;

But from the prized auxiliary,
To Mary came no answering cry.
Foiled by the Fair—but not dismayed,
Edmond forsakes the leafy shade,
And where the ripples kiss the strand,
He gains once more her treasured hand;
Yes! charmer of my heart, I own,
A potent spell is round me thrown;
But Mary, 'twas thy guileless art,
That wove the spell that rules my heart;
Oh! rule it still, bewitching fair,
Oh! still let me my fetters wear;
I would not rend of that fond chain,
Thyself has forged, one link to gain
Earth's brightest crown—Then let me tell,
The hopes thy captive's bosom swell.
Oh! spare me, cried the blushing fair,
Brave, generous youth, thy suit forbear,
A father's life in peril saved,
At risk of thine—A home bereaved,
Its every hope with gloom o'ercast,
By thee restored to bliss at last;
Our hearts our benefactor bless,
And own their deep indebtedness;
A debt so great, our latest day,
Can never, never half repay.
Alas! the tender boon you crave,
Unworthy I, to be your slave.
Too lately has my breast betrayed
Its hopes by former memory's swayed;
I dare not act untruthful part,

I cannot school my wayward heart.
Her face with crimson blushes dyed,
She turned away, her tears to hide;
Then Mary first became aware,
Of other witness to her care,
And feelings strong, beyond control,
Oppressed her sad, affrighted soul.
For busy rumors tidings spread,
Long since, that Hannah Bawn was dead;
She loved in life her kindly face,
But now she flees her sought embrace,
And Mary's scream the hill alarms,
Whilst rushing in the stranger's arms.
Nay, gentle maiden, do not fear,
This is a harmless spaewife here;
This morn I gave her ring of gold,
And she my book of fate unroll'd.
Has times unfolding, Hannah cried,
My praise and prophesy belied?
From her protector, Mary Sprung,
And to that aged bosom clung?
Hannah, forgive my wild'red fear,
Oh! what of Edmond? Hast'ning here
He sends by me thy grace to sue,
And old time memories to renew;
This ring—thou know'st its device strange—
Like his true breast, it knows no change:
The black wolf by the lamb controll'd,
This, his ancestral crest of old—
Ere recreant sons their sires denied,
And changed their name their guilt to hide.

Soon Edmond shall the name restore,
To the green shades of Goreymore.
Alas! mine eyes grow bleared and dim,
Trembles my hand, my senses swim;
Here, stranger, place this golden band,
For Edmond, on this maiden's hand,
And by thy faith and honor, swear,
Till Edmond come to shield the Fair.
Ah! reckless muse, from curious eyes,
Our story's closing scene disguise;
Veil thou from vulgar gaze and vain,
Love's holacust and secret fane,
Nor let gross heart nor footstep rude,
On that chaste, blissful scene intrude.
The Friar's Curse, long held in dread,
Behold its final problem read.
So fancy breaks her wizard spell,
So breathes the muse her last farewell;
And I, life's contest to renew,
Now bid old scenes and muse, Adieu!

END OF FIFTH CANTO.

NOTES TO CANTO FIRST.

NOTE 1.—"When turning from the surging Foyle."

Lough Foyle forms the Eastern boundary of the ancient territory of Inishowen.

I cannot better introduce my story than by giving a description of the road over which my hero has to pass, taken from a most interesting and valuable little work, entitled: "Inishowen—Its History, Traditions and Antiquities," compiled by "Maghtochair," and published in the Londonderry Journal office in 1867, as follows: "At Quigley's Point, on the leading road from Derry to Moville, and about midway between them, a road strikes off nearly at right angles; it runs up the slope of the hill due west for nearly a mile, and then turns sharply to the north, leaving at this point the Clonilly National School, embosomed in the furze, unprofitably gay, and in its onward course passes through Glentogher, Carn, Malin, and eventually terminates at the sea near Malin Head From the turn near the school the incline is gradually downward for about three miles, where it enters a narrow gorge or pass; here the mountains on each side seem standing up in stern sullenness, and bidding a grim defiance to their opposite neighbors. Before the days of macadamizing, 'ere that vicious circle, the surveyor's ring, was known or invented, a bridle road led through here, and along its beaten and devious path horse and foot pedestrians and equestrians were wont to make their way from or to the lower bottom of Inishowen. The neat bridge which now spans the roaring torrent of the hills, was not there, but instead a line of collosal stepping-stones ran across the ford, which means of transit was, in the language of the day, termed a *Cloghan*. The stepping-stones have vanished with the age to which they belonged, but the name, still more enduring, attaches to the place. Before crossing the Cloghan in our downward journey, we all at once, and most unexpectedly, meet a luxuriant plantation, in the very depths of the mountain wilderness. The trees are birch and Norway firs, larch, elms and beeches; in the midst there is an excellent farm-house, in good occupation. Crossing the Cloghan, a few minutes walk will bring us to Ardnapriest (from which the great serpent was expelled by St. Patrick). We now enter Glentogher, where

Oft from out a tiny spout
The bowl of Bacchus flowed.

And well suited is the glen for such a purpose—abundance of water in every part coming gushing down from unfailing fountains in the hills, sparkling and pure as on the morn of Creation, with hides and haunts that the keenest experts have as yet failed to discover. Glennagannon, or the glen beyond, in allusion to the former one, because it lies beyond the hill to the east, is a kind of *cul de sac*, being hemmed in by mountains on all sides, save to the north, where it opens on the plains of Maghtoher. The leading roads terminate at its inner extremity, beyond which is a wide extended district of bog, reaching to the confines of Carrickmaquigley on the Foyle."

To the book from which this description is taken I shall be indebted for the greater portion of the notes which I may use in this volume.

NOTE 2.—"THE FRIAR'S CURSE."—The Friar's Curse is founded on a tradition of what occurred in the family of one of the O'Doherty's, whose residence lay in the valley of Lag.

The legend says, when pursued he sought his father's house, and gained the paternal blessing and fled the place, running backward for at least a mile over the yielding sand to where his boat lay. The place of embarkation still bears the name of "Rhun-na-wad," (in English, "the long run.") His pursuers had to cross his track to reach the house; they traced his footsteps there, but were unable to discover any leaving it, and before the ruse was found out, O'Doherty's heir was beyond their reach.

NOTE 3.—"I saw it then, my child, its sickening gore."

The gift of second sight and Palmistry was, even in my boyish days, a popular belief, and according to the tradition, was possessed by the father of young O'Doherty.

NOTE 4.—"GO KILL A COOK."—Such were the remedies recommended, to see if the spilling of the blood of those animals would free the hand from the stains visible to the eye of the seer.

NOTE 5.—"Pass thou this day at Great St. Columb's shrine."

In the parish of Clonmany, on the opposite shore of Strabreagy, a church was founded by St. Columb in the sixth century, connected with a rich Monastery; the church is still occupied by the Episcopalians.

NOTE 6.—"Where Donagh's granite crosses grey with age."

My memory deceived me when I wrote this. I had supposed there were two crosses. The source of my historical notes furnishes the following description of the cross:

"Beside the Church stands a stone cross, more than six feet high, hewn out of a solid block, and ornamented with numerous scrolls and shamrocks; on each side of it is a square pillar, and on three of the sides of each of these pillars is engraved the figure of a human head; on that pillar which is next the public road, there is upon one side, besides the head, also a heart, and the heart is above the head. The Church was founded by St. Patrick on a Sunday, and named by him Domnah-Mor-Muge-Tochuir, in commemoration, it seems, of the day on which he founded it, in the vale of the causeway; from this the parish of Donagh derives its name, and the Church still stands on the same spot, though it has undergone alterations and repairs at various periods, lastly in 1812. The Church is now in possession of the Episcopalians, together with its ancient bell, cast in Italy, with this pious legend beneath its cross,

'Sancta Maria, Ora pro nobis.'"

NOTE 7.—"Strike, son of Denmark, for thy father's fame."

Feardarrig means red-man, and red-haired persons were supposed to have Danish blood in their veins.

NOTE 8.—"The guilt thy soul affrights in Columb Kill's rude cell."

On the Island of Torry, about nine miles from the main land, the Saint had a cell to which he frequently retired to meditate.

NOTE 9.—"Within his cell of stone in sanctity."

The "Friar's house," as it was called, was built entirely of stone against and below the projection of a rock that formed one of its walls; it was located on the farm of Shane Friel, and in good preservation when I last saw it, nearly thirty years ago.

NOTE 10.—"All duty days, all Chiefry hence forbear."

The custom of working duty days for the landlord, principally cutting turf, still lingered in the manor in my early day. The tribute of chiefry was not exacted in the vicinity where I was born, within my memory.

NOTE 11.—"Three holy wells are flowing there."

Doonhill, at the head of the strand of Strabreagy, overlooks these wells; and notwithstanding that my latest witness says there are *two* wells, I must still cling to the number engraven on the tablets of my memory, although I may be in error.

NOTE 12.—"Brazils from Ballyhillion's ben."

Often have I listened enwrapt in wonder, to the description of that enchanted and magnificent landscape, that, according to the tradition, arises visible to the material eye once only in each seven years. The act of fortitude, wherein lies the talismanic spell, which will redeem the charmed territory from the ocean beneath which it lies, has escaped my memory; and as any inaccuracy in my statement must necessarily prove fatal to the adventurer in his perilous undertaking, I must refer him to those, who, on the rugged slopes of Ballyhillion, still hand down unerring from generation to generation, the hazardous conditions on which the awe-struck beholder may attempt the reclamation of the Brazils.

NOTE 13.—"And Donnah Dearrig learned and wise."

Donaghy Dearrig of the Ben Gorms, to whose prophetic lore I have often listened with a feeling of reverence and awe, may have been a lineal descendant of his elder namesake.

NOTE 14.—"Last Hallowmass a hunstman bold."

When, in my youthful days, with others of my companions, I crossed Cranny going to or returning from the Chapel of Lag, as we invariably did in the summer-time, should any of our companions who, for the first time, "dared the dizzy height," show symptoms of fear, his courage was stimulated by the assurance that Billy Ban Bogs of Lag had ridden his black mare over the same path. Such was the belief of us boys at that time. As I was not an eye-witness of the exploit, I will, to save my reputation for exactness, mark the story—Apocriphal.

NOTE 15.—"Benevnue's Fairy King, they say."

The flight of the herds over the mountains and valleys, driven by some invisible power, the sounds of conflict in the air, and all alluded to in the text, were a popular tradition among my native glens.

NOTE 16.—"A specter ship, her sails unfurled."

Science has long since divested the mirage of its miraculous origin, and portentious character.

NOTE 17.—"No Ban she gave her warning wail."

The office of the Banshe being so well understood, I will only add, with us she was acknowledged a former member of the family, the death of one of whom her wail prognosticated or mourned, she having been taken away by the fairies when a child. So firm was this belief held by one of my female ancestors, whose span of life extended over four score years, and who died over thirty years ago. I have heard her assert that no male head of her father's family died, until Sally's plaintive voice in Kena preceded the event.

NOTE 18.—"Tho' Kelly's wraith was seen in Drung."

The wraith (or, as we pronounce it, wrath), was the resemblance of one who was still alive and in health, but absent from the place of vision. It, I believe, prognosticated a sudden and untimely death to the party whose image it assumed. The sound of hammers and the death bell alluded to in the text, are all of the same class, and relate to the sudden end of some one or more of the family whose ears have heard the ominous sounds.

NOTES TO CANTO SECOND.

NOTE 1.—"Slieve Snaght, 'tis thine by lofty claim."

Slieve Snaght (in English, Snow Hill,) is the highest of the mountains that, like an army of Giants, encircle the valley, and rises from the shores of Strabreagy to an altitude, according to Bett's map of Ireland, of 2,232 feet above sea level

NOTE 2.—"Like that old serpent, huge and black."

There is a tradition that at Ardnapaest, in Glentogher, there existed a great serpent, the scourge and terror of all who passed that way, then, as now, one of the principal thoroughfares of the country. No earthly power could dislodge him from his stronghold. At the solicitations of the people, St. Patrick took the matter in hand, combated and pierced him with his pastoral staff, and, bleeding as he was, compelled him by exorcisms to take his departure. Off the fearful thing crawled; nor did he stop till he arrived at Lough Derg, the waters of which he dyed red with his blood. The lake became the serpent's grave, and from the shedding of its blood therein it obtained the name which it still bears.

NOTE 3.—"Since Daniel of the silver tongue."

Dan O'Doherty, an amateur harper who resided at Keenagh, having received an insult at the house of one of the strangers then in possession of the heritage of his forefathers, by being offered pay for his enlivening the company with his harp, abruptly left, broke his beloved instrument on his arrival home, and was never known to play again.

NOTE 4.—"As dies that bird whose death illumes."

The Phœnix.

NOTES TO CANTO FOURTH.

NOTE 1.—"And matchless all; but Oraray."

The Demesne of Jonn Harvey, Esq., of Malin Hall, Oraray being the name of the Quarterland—having never seen the word written, I may have mistaken the orthography.

NOTE 2.—"Thy haunted hawthorn by the sea."

This tree grew on the northern bank of the stream on which the mill of Malin was built, at its confluence with the waters of Strabreagy, and was known to old and young as a "gentle bush."

NOTE ?.—"Great Fairy King of Inishowen."

The hills of Knockamenny, Knockglass, Lag and Gorey, and even the Gulf of Strabreagy, were regarded, time out of mind, as fairy or *gentle* ground. The fairy King of that district, as well as of the Lough, was Niall-na-ard, or Neil of the heights. In deference to the authority from which I gather this note, I must lower the dignity of my King, Oughie, to that of Viceroy.

ERRATUM.

Page 8, line 21—For spaned, read spanned.
Page 10, line 27—For vail, read veil.
Page 16—After the first line read Owen Roe O'Neil, Prince of Tirowm.
Page 22, line 1—For near, read ne'er.
Page 24, verse xvii, line 7—For it, read its.
Page 25, line 2—For land, read band.
Page 33, verse xli, line 5—For an, read and. Same verse, line 9—After clans insert a.
Page 35, verse xlvii, line 9—For no, read now.
Page 40, verse ii, line 6—For see, read flee.
Page 88, line 3—For win his, read won its.
Page 193, line 25—After "but he would", insert the word "hear."
Page 250, line 11—For dereed, read decreed.

www.ingramcontent.com/pod-product-compliance
Lightning Source LLC
LaVergne TN
LVHW010238110826
845151LV00004B/1332

* 9 7 8 1 4 2 5 5 2 3 7 5 6 *